Soar with me

Soar with me

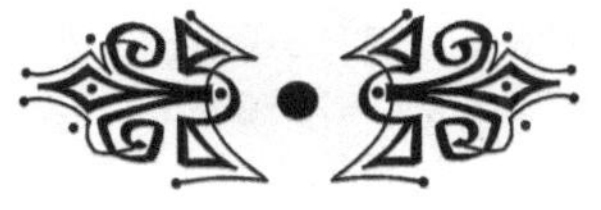

WALLI ANTONIE ZAMORANO

Library of Congress Control Number: 2022900758

HARDBACK: 978-1-957575-06-3
PAPERBACK: 978-1-957575-05-6
EBOOK: 978-1-957575-07-0

Ordering Information:

For orders and inquiries, please contact:
1-888-404-1388
www.goldtouchpress.com
book.orders@goldtouchpress.com

Printed in the United States of America

Introduction

It is my prayer that you will be blessed by reading these poems. I cannot boast of a special gift, because I know the Lord is the author of all of the poems.

I am so grateful that He has given me the privilege to put them on paper and to share them with others.

Some are prophecies in the form of poems. Some are pure praise and adoration; others are exhortation. They have all been a blessing to my own soul.

May you find insight and answers to some of your questions in these scribal writings.

All the poems are in agreement with the Word of God.

The Lord had me search out passages in the Bible that would confirm the message of the poem and include them for edification. I have added a section for making notes of the thoughts the Lord may give you while meditating on the poem or scripture.

The Scripture is taken from the King James Version of the Bible unless otherwise indicated.

Walli Antonie Zamorano

Come Up Higher

He who dwells in the Secret Place
Of the Most High shall abide
Under the shadow of the Almighty

Psalm 91:1

My Meditation

IN THE SECRET PLACE

O Precious Lord
Spending time with you right here
In the secret place
Far removed from doubt and fear
Fills my heart with highest praise
O Precious Lord, when you draw near
There is a change in the atmosphere
It is as if any moment now
A host of angels will appear
To meet You face to face
To feel your warm embrace
Makes me want to stay
Right here all of my living days
Like the early morning dew
Falls on the roses each day anew
So this time alone with you
Floods my soul through and through
It is in the early morning hour
I need a brand new touch from you
A refreshing shower
Of the Holy Spirit's Power
That will last the whole day through
O what Joy will flood your heart When you make time to come apart
To spend time with Him alone Kneeling down, close to His Throne

A Thousand Songs

There are a thousand songs yet to be sung
In adoration of the Holy One
There are not enough words of praise
To thank Him for His Mercy and His Grace

There are a thousand souls yet to be won
Who will accept the sacrifice of God's only Son
And will be cleansed by His blood from all their sin
So that the Holy Spirit can come in

There are a thousand battles to be fought
How to win the war; we have been taught
The high praises in our mouth
And the two-edged sword in our hand
The enemy of our soul will not be able to withstand

There are a thousand Amen's to be raised
By all the ones who through the ages have been saved
They have finished their course and won the crown
And on the right hand of the throne
They will sit down

There are a thousand thanks to be expressed
From all who openly the name of Jesus have confessed
Even if a martyr's death they'll have to face
They'll be witnesses for Christ in every place

There is not any time to waste we must make haste
One more soul to win, so the final harvest can come in
Jesus' reign on earth can finally begin

Scripture

*Fear none of those things that thou shalt suffer; behold,
the devil shall cast some of you into prison, that ye may
be tried; and ye shall have tribulation ten days, be thou
faithful unto death, and I will give thee the crown of life.*
Revelation 2:10

*And it shall come to pass, that whosoever shall
call on the Name of the Lord shall be saved.*
Acts 2: 21

*If thou shalt confess with thy mouth the Lord Jesus
and shalt believe in thine heart, that God hath
raised him from the dead, thou shalt be saved.*
Romans 10:9

Abba Father

Abba Father, is what I cry
As I lift my face up to the sky
With my hands upraised
I offer You my highest praise

You are God There is no other
There is no one like you
To you all praise is due
God Most High

So far and yet so nigh
You set the stars into place
Yet don't forget to kiss my face
You are the Almighty

When in your secret place I hide
And under the shadow
Of your wings abide
Then safety from the storm
You will provide

You rule supremely over all
Yet you can hear me when I call
Your eyes can see all that I do
Father, that's why I am praising you

Scripture

*For ye have not received the spirit of bondage again
to fear; but ye have received the Spirit of adoption,
whereby we cry, Abba Father.*
Romans 8: 15

*He that dwelleth in the secret place of the Most
High shall abide under the shadow of the Almighty.*
Psalm 91:1

*Remember the former things of old: for I am
God, and there is none else; I am God, and there
is none like me.*
Isaiah 46:9

Adoration

Lord, I come before You now
in humble adoration bow
You are the King of all the earth
Before you made the angels
You were there

When with all that you had created
No fellowship You found
You formed man out of the dust of the ground
You walked with Adam in the cool of the night
God and man together, O, what a sight

This man that God had made
Disobeyed and fell from Grace

In the fullness of time You sent Your Son
To bare the sins of everyone
His innocent blood he shed on a tree
To provide Salvation for all humanity

I want to laugh and at the same time cry
As prostrate before Your throne I lie
"Lift up your head," You whisper in my ear
As You are drawing near
When man confesses his sin, our fellowship can begin
For the Praise of my Glory, I have created him

Just as in the Garden it began
When You first walked with man
So shall it be for all eternity
"Will you walk in the Garden with me?" I hear You say
Praise, Praise, exalted Praise forever I will raise

Scripture

So God created man in His own image, in the image of God created He him; male and female created He them.
Genesis 1:27

But of the tree of the knowledge of good and evil, thou shalt not eat of it: for in the that thou eatest thereof thou shalt surely die.
Genesis 2:18

Therefore the Lord God sent him forth from the garden of Eden to till the ground from whence he was taken.
Genesis 3:23

Behold Your Creator

When you lift your eyes on high
And you gaze into the sky
You will see the splendor of His Majesty
Stars and Planets forming Galaxies

As you travel in your mind
You wonder what lies behind
It can only be the dwelling place of Him
Who created everything

Oh, how we become so small
As we behold the splendor of it all
Could it be true, that this Almighty God
Is looking down on me and you

It is too awesome to comprehend
That this Creator of all would send
His only begotten Son to rescue men

We must believe, it is true
God alone can make all things new
He is all powerful and all knowing
He knows where we've been
And where we're going
All I can do is cry out to Him
Lord, forgive me for my sin

When you meditate day and night
It will lead you in the way that's right
Let us worship Him, He is the only One

The Great I Am, the Holy One And let us
give honor to Jesus His Son

Scripture

*In the beginning God created the heaven
and the earth.
Genesis 1:1*

*Ah, Lord God, thou hast made the heaven
and the earth by thy great power and
stretched out arm, and there is nothing too
hard for thee.
Jeremiah 32:18*

*For God sent not his son into the world
to condemn the world; but that the world
through him might be saved.
John 3:17*

WALLI ANTONIE ZAMORANO

Do You Know The King

Do you know the King
Who created everything
Jesus is His Name
Forever He will reign

Do you know the King
Who rules over everything
He controls the sun and moon
Separating night from noon

Do you know the King
Who gave up everything
He came to this earth
Through a humble birth

Do you know the King
Of whom the angels sing

Do you know the King
Who wants us to bring
The sacrifice of Praise
With holy hands upraised

Now you know the King,
Bow down and worship Him
Your praise and adoration
Will become His habitation

Nothing can separate us from His Love
we've been purchased by His Blood
Glory to Him alone
Who sits upon the throne

Scripture

The Lord is king for ever and ever, the heathen are perished out of the land.
Psalm 10:16

Who is the king of Glory? The Lord strong and mighty, the Lord mighty in battle. Who is this King of Glory? the Lord of Hosts He is the King of Glory.
Psalm 24:8

Tell ye the daughters of Sion, behold thy King cometh unto thee, meek and sitting on an ass, and a colt the foal of an ass.
Matthew 21:5

Hosanna

Hosanna, Hosanna
Open up the gates
So the King of Glory
May come in

Hosanna, Hosanna
Give Him Praise
Let the tabernacle of David
Again be raised

Hosanna, Hosanna
Let us declare together
God is good and His Mercy
Endureth forever

Hosanna, Hosanna
Watch and pray
The Lord is coming back
On the appointed day

Hosanna, Hosanna
Praise the risen Lord
The glory train
Will be leaving soon

You better get aboard

Scripture

*Lift up your heads, O ye gates; even lift them
up ye everlasting doors, and the King of Glory
shall come in.*

*Who is this King of Glory?
The Lord of Hosts, he is the King of Glory.
Psalm 24: 9,10*

*After this I will return and again build the tabernacle
of David, which is fallen down, and I will build again
the ruins thereof, and I will set it up.
Acts 15:16*

Let Joy Arise

Let Joy arise in your soul
It will make you whole
Joy is a wonderful thing
Its power works deep within

New strength begins to flow
Your confidence will grow
Your faith will soar
To heights its never reached before

You'll mount up on eagles wings
Freedom from bondage it brings
Joy will give you the victory
Over the fiery darts from the enemy

His Joy He'll give to you
It will help you through
Every trial and test
And give your spirit rest

This Joy you will find
Only through a renewed mind
In the one who is born from above
And walks in the Father's love

It is your secret weapon
It will make things happen
Above all things be wise
And let His Joy in you arise

Scripture

*Whom having not seen, ye love, in whom, though
now ye see him not, yet believing, ye rejoice with
joy unspeakable and full of Glory.*
Peter 1:8

*....for this day is holy unto the Lord; neither be ye
sorry; for the Joy of the Lord is your strength.*
Nehemiah 8:10

*My brethren count it all joy when ye fall into
divers temptations.*
James 1:2

Let Praise Arise

When you let Praise arise in your heart
I'll give you a fresh start
Everything will be new
Like the early morning dew

If you want to come up higher
Praise is what I require
It will give you the victory
Over the attack of the enemy

Out of the mouths of babes
I have ordained Praise
The avenger must cease
And his captives release

When you praise Me in your darkest hour
I will visit you with My power
The place might start to shake
And the earth begin to quake

When you bring the Sacrifice of Praise
My Presence will come into that place
Holy laughter you might hear
When the saints are drawing near

When you enter My courts with Praise
and seek My Face
Then I'll give you overcoming power
For the final hour

Scripture

*Enter his gates with thanksgiving and his
courts with praise; be thankful unto him,
and bless his Name.*
Psalm 100:4

*Praise ye the Lord. Praise God in the sanctuary
praise him in the firmament of his power.*

*Praise him for his mighty acts; praise him
according to his excellent greatness.*

*Let everything that has breath praise the Lord.
Praise ye the Lord.*
Psalm 150

Now Is The Time

Now is the Time
To bow before our King
An offering of Thanksgiving to bring
He is worthy of our adoration
He is King over every nation

Now is the Time
To sing the high praises to the Lord
And wield the two-edged sword
The Word of God will bind the enemy
And bring the saints the victory

Now is the Time
To come before His Majesty
To blend our voices in harmony
To make just one sound to be heard
And see His Glory kiss the earth

Now is the Time
To clap our hands and dance and shout
And watch Him bring the captives out
The blood of Jesus
Is the power that frees us

Now is the Time
To watch and pray, and occupy
And to keep our eyes on the sky
Soon we will see the Lord
In the clouds above
Gathering His Bride

The object of His LOVE

Scripture

Let them praise his name in the dance, let them sing praises to him with the timbrel and harp.

Let the high praises of God be in their mouth and a two-edged sword in their hands
Psalm 149

For the Lord himself shall descend from heaven with a shout, with the voice of the archangel and with the trump of God; and the dead in Christ shall rise first.
I Thess. 4:16

 Walli Antonie Zamorano

Raise Your Praise

Are you weary
Are you tired of running the race
Just lift up your head and raise your Praise

Praise will bring you out, just give the Lord a shout
It is the weapon for this hour, it'll bring down God's power
The High Praises of the Lord are your spiritual sword

You must take hold of this revelation
if you want to walk in the Joy of your Salvation
Joy is the currency to bring you out of your misery

His Joy will lift you higher
Out of your innermost being will flow living water
like a mighty stream. It will revive your broken dream
When you let Praise arise, it will silence the devil's lies
The kingdom of darkness will be shattered
the enemy will be scattered
When your Praises will make one sound
God will even shake the ground

This Joy the whole world
Will see on the people's faces
from all the different races
Black, brown, yellow and white
All of them will reflect His light

His favor will come on all
Who praise Him great and small
In God's Love they will walk

Of His wonders daily talk
When you raise your Praise
He'll give you Grace

Scripture

You shall also decree a thing, and it shall

be established unto thee: and the light shall
shine upon thy ways.
Job 22:28

Restore unto me the Joy of my Salvation;
and uphold me with thy free spirit.
Psalm 51:12

Let the high praises of God be in their
mouth and a two-edged sword in their hand.
Psalm 149:6

WALLI ANTONIE ZAMORANO

Rejoice Everyone

Rejoice, rejoice
And hearken to His voice
Incline your ear, and you will hear
A mighty rushing wind draw near

Rejoice, rejoice!
Pay no attention to the noise
Of all the enemy's distractions
Keep your eyes on the Lord
Let the spoken Word be your sword

Rejoice, rejoice
While you still have a choice
If you want to stay the course
The Word of God must be your only source
All else is but a clever lie
Follow it and you will surely die

Rejoice, rejoice
And again I say rejoice
It may be morning, night or noon
The coming of the Lord is soon
Cleanse your hearts today
Repent and pray

Rejoice, rejoice
Can you hear the joyful noise
The blood washed saints in Glory
Are singing the redemption story

Scripture

*And suddenly there came a sound from heaven
as of a rushing mighty wind, and it filled all the
house where they were sitting.*
Acts 2:2

*And take the helmet of salvation, and the sword
of the Spirit, which is the Word of God.*
Ephesians 6:17

*For yourselves know perfectly that the day of the
Lord so cometh as a thief in the night.*
I Thessalonians

The Joy Of The Lord

Let me tell you the story
of Joy unspeakable and full of Glory
When you give your life to Him your story will begin
You'll have a brand new start when the kingdom of God
"Righteousness, Peace and Joy", comes into your heart
Never again to depart

Joy is a reservoir deep within
When we start praising Jesus
An overflowing river will begin
It will come bubbling out, sometimes with a "shout"
This Joy will flood your soul. It will make you whole
It is a never ending force. Heaven is its source

When tests and trials come your way
"Count it all Joy" the scriptures say
It is a law; what we want to possess
We must first with our mouth confess

When you are sad and you know
That your Joy has ceased to flow
And in your throat you feel a lump
You must "prime the pump"
Just bring a sacrifice of Praise to start
And pretty soon new Joy will flood your heart

Even though you might be weeping
This Joy of Jesus keeps on sweeping
Over your soul all night until the early morning light
New strength you will find in your body and your mind

Scripture

*Looking unto Jesus the author and finisher
of our Faith; who for the Joy that was set
before him, endured the cross, despising
the shame, and is set down at the right hand
of the throne of God.*
Hebrews 12:2

*By him therefore let us offer the sacrifice of
Praise to God continually, that is the fruit of
our lips giving thanks to his Name.*
Hebrews 13:15

*My brethren count it all Joy when ye fall into
divers temptations.*
James 1:2

The Key To Victory

O, my children can't you see
I've given you the victory
Your battle has been won
Through the sacrifice of My Son

The enemy has been defeated
At My right hand My Son is seated
Give Him Glory, give Him Praise
To Him alone the banner raise

Do you need the victory?
Praise and worship is the key
It opens and shuts the doors you cannot see

When trouble wants to stay
Praise Me anyway
When you're down and out
Give a shout
Praising Me will bring you out

King David caught this revelation
When He danced before the ark
With all his might
His Praise became My habitation
I showed him how to win the fight

My Son will come back to you as king
After the restitution of all things
He alone will sit on David's throne

There will be great jubilation
On Zion's hill a joyful celebration
When the people shout in one accord
Holiness unto the Lord

Scripture

*Looking unto Jesus the author and finisher of
our faith; who for the joy that was set before
him endured the cross, despising the shame, and
is set down at the right hand of the throne of God.
Hebrews 12:2*

*And to the angel of the church in Philadelphia
write; These things saith he that is holy, he
that is true, he that hath the key of David, he
that openeth and no man shutteth and shutteth
and no man openeth.
Revelation 3:7*

WALLI ANTONIE ZAMORANO

The Tabernacle Of David

When David was Israel's king
He established a brand new thing
He built a tent on Zion's hill
For God with His presence to fill
He brought the Ark of God inside
No longer in the Holy of Holy's to hide

Twenty-four hours a day musicians
Were appointed to play
The Levites were anointed to minister
To the Lord and pray
The trumpets were sounding day and night
O, what a glorious sight

This form of worship was a glimpse into eternity
A foreshadow of what is yet to be
Can you see the angels around the Throne
Bowing down to Him alone
The chorus of the redeemed chiming in
Their adoration and exaltation to bring

When Jesus' Blood was spent
The veil in the temple was rent
He died for our sins to atone
Now we have access to His Throne

When the saints are worshipping in one accord
Making only one sound to be heard
Blending their voices in perfect harmony
Then we will be tuned into Heaven's frequency
And the tabernacle of David
Will be raised for all eternity

Scripture

*In that day will I raise up the tabernacle of
David that is fallen, and close up the breaches
thereof and I will raise up his ruins, and I will
build it as the days of old.*
Amos 9:11

*After this I will return and again build the
tabernacle of David, which is fallen down;
and I will build again the ruins thereof, and
I will set it up.*
Acts 15:16

The Trinity

Father, Holy Spirit and the Son
We adore you Three- in -One
As it is in heaven, so let your Kingdom come

Father, you loved us so much you send your Son
To become the sacrificial Lamb
To die for the sins of everyone

Jesus, we lift up your Name
We are so grateful that you came
You paid the ultimate price
So we can be born twice

We are all born of the flesh, conceived in sin
We need to be born of the Spirit
who makes us new within
We must be washed in the blood, the cleansing flood
And be forgiven for our sin, our new life to begin

Holy Spirit, you came at Pentecost
To send us out to win the lost
We need you in this final hour
To come and demonstrate your Power

Holy, holy, holy is our triune God
He is full of mercy and compassion
He is the Truth, the Way and the Life
In His presence we are revived

Scripture

There are three that bear record in heaven
the Father, the Word, and the Holy Ghost
and these three are one.
I John 5:7

And when the day of Pentecost was fully come,
they were all with one accord in one place.
And suddenly there came a sound from
heaven as of a rushing mighty wind, and it
filled all the house where they were sitting
And they were all filled with the Holy Ghost,
and began to speak with other tongues, as
the Spirit gave them utterance.
Acts 2: 1,2,4

To The Glory Of His Grace

Lord Jesus, we thank You that You came
And that You have given us Your Name
Lord, we need You in this hour
We cannot fight the enemy without Your power

O Lord, we need your Mercy now
Humbly in your presence we bow
Please, send your cleansing fire again
And make us pure within

Please forgive us for our sin
We need Your strategy to win
Lord, we lift our Praise
To the Glory of Your Grace

Our weapons are mighty through God
With His armor we are shod
With the sword of the Spirit in our hand
We are conquering the land

We are the people of the Lord
Marching on in one accord
Our banner to the Lord of Host's we raise
To the Glory of His Grace.

The enemy cannot hide
He cannot stand against the tide
Of Jesus' Blood
That overtakes him like a flood

We have fought the good fight
And finished our race
Forever we shall lift our Praise
To the Glory of His Grace

Scripture

But who may abide in the day of His coming?
and who shall stand when he appeareth?
for he is like a refiner's fire, and like fuller's soap.

And He shall sit as a refiner and purifier of silver,
and he shall purify the sons of Levi, and purge them
as gold and silver, that they may offer unto the
Lord an offering in righteousness.
Malachi 3:2,3

I have fought a good fight. I have finished the
course, I have kept the faith.
II Timothy 4:7

Unspeakable Joy

There's Joy, Joy, Joy, unspeakable Joy
In the heart of the redeemed
Everything is new
Like the early morning dew
The old man is dead
You're a brand new creature instead

There's Joy, Joy, Joy, unspeakable Joy
In the heart of the redeemed
Jesus died for you! Believe it! It is true
His precious blood He gave
Our wretched souls to save

There's Joy, Joy, Joy, unspeakable Joy
In the heart of the redeemed
There's healing in His wings.
Deliverance He brings
You're broken heart He'll mend
His love for you will never end

There's Joy, Joy, Joy, unspeakable Joy
In the heart of the redeemed
Hear the trumpet blow!
He's coming back, I know
The time is drawing near
When in the clouds He shall appear

Scripture

Whom having not seen ye love; in whom,
though now ye see him not, yet believing,
ye rejoice with Joy unspeakable and full
of Glory.
I Peter 1:8

But the fruit of the Spirit is love, joy, peace,
longsuffering, gentleness, goodness; faith.
meekness, temperance: against such there
is no law.
Galatians 5:22

Worship Me

Come into My gates with thanksgiving
Enter My courts with praise
Come before Me with singing
In holy worship your voices raise

While I am watching from above
beholding the expressions of your love
A sweet sound will come into My ear
And I'll be drawing near

When your voices blend in perfect harmony
And your praises become a symphony
When you're all in one accord

And someone sings the "Song of the Lord
Then I will come down into your midst
And will sit down and take My place
Upon your throne of praise

With My right hand My scepter I'll extend
It will be My pleasure to open up My treasure
Then I will distribute My gifts among the crowd
Some will receive their healing, some will prophesy
Some will burst out laughing
And others will break down and cry
Some will shout, while others dance about

O, what a Joy it is for Me
To be amidst My family

Scripture

*Shout for Joy unto the Lord all the earth
worship the Lord with gladness. Come
before Him with joyful songs. Know that
the Lord is God. It is HE who made us
and we are His people the sheep of his pasture.
Enter his gates
with thanksgiving and His courts with praise,
give thanks to Him and praise His Name.
For the Lord is good and His love endures
forever; his faithfulness endures through
all generations.
Psalm 100*

Worship The King

Can you see the King upon the throne
We must worship Him alone
He is the Creator of everything you see
His rule will be for all eternity

All Honor and Glory belong to Him
He is the King of kings
He rules with Righteousness and Power
He is our strength and high tower

He does not dwell in a building with a steeple
He inhabits the Praises of His people
When our Praise and Worship exalt the Son
We have built Him a throne to sit upon

His scepter He'll extend to all
Who will humbly obey His call
He freely distributes gifts among His own
And makes His glorious Presence known

The angels hail the Lamb upon the throne
Who came to earth for mankind to atone
They do not comprehend the pain
That He endured when He was slain

The Lamb has become the Lion
He will come and rule in Zion
The old dragon He has put away
For a thousand years in the pit to stay

Scripture

*Now unto the King eternal, immortal invisible,
the only wise God, be Honor and Glory for
ever and ever, Amen
I Timothy 1:17*

*Which in his times he shall shew, who is the
blessed and only Potentate, the King of kings,
and the Lord of lords.
I Timothy 6:15*

*And He has on His vesture and on His thigh a
name written, KING OF KINGS AND LORD
OF LORDS.
Revelations 19:16*

Why Do They Shout

Somebody tell me
Who are these peculiar people
And why do they have to shout
What is their excitement all about

They're acting in the strangest way
I can't understand a word they say
It seems like they drank too much
I was told, religion was just a crutch

Although it doesn't have much appeal
What these people have is real
There is joy on each face
And laughter fills the place

It seems to be contagious
There are people of all different ages
Even the children are dancing about
And some of them are falling out

If you really want to know
What makes their faces glow
And why they are demonstrating such love
It's because they've been born from above

Everyone on earth must have a second birth
If they want to go to heaven
God, the Father sent His only Son
Who died for the sins of everyone

When you ask Him into your heart
He'll give you a brand new start
And you will find out
Why these peculiar people shout

Scripture

*But ye are a chosen generation a royal priesthood,
a holy nation a peculiar people; that ye should
shew forth the praises of him who hath called you
out of darkness into his marvelous light.*
I Peter 2:9

*Jesus answered and said unto him, Verily,
verily, I say unto thee, except a man be born
again, he cannot see the kingdom of God.*
John 3:3

WALLI ANTONIE ZAMORANO

Soar With The Eagle

But they that wait upon the Lord
shall renew their strength;
they shall mount up with wings as eagles;
they shall run, and not be weary;
they shall walk and not faint.

Isaiah 40:31

A Clarion Call

Come to me
Come to the altar and worship me
Gather around
You are standing on Holy Ground
No more weeping, no more blame
I've delivered you from shame
No more sickness, no more pain
For these the Lamb of God was slain

Enter in! Let the celebration begin
Refreshing times are here
For all who will draw near
Some are young; some are old
Some are hot, and some are cold
Let the truth be told
They are all part of My fold

You must stay sober
The battle is not over
Walk circumspectly
Think before you speak
It will bring victory or defeat
When you gather in My Name
And your confession is the same
When you all come into perfect unity
Then great exploits you will see
Can you hear
My latter rain is drawing near
It won't just be a shower
It will be a deluge of my power
Watch and pray
You must prepare the way
So you will not miss My visitation
That will come to every nation

WALLI ANTONIE ZAMORANO

Scripture

*Repent therefore and be converted, that your sins
may be blotted out, when the times of refreshing
shall come from the presence of the Lord.*

*And he shall send Jesus Christ, which before
was preached unto you:*

*Whom the heaven must receive until the times
of restitution of all things, which God hath
spoken by the mouth of all his holy prophets
since the world began.*
Acts 3: 19-21

Empty Vessels

I am looking for empty vessels
To pour Myself through
To release a new anointing
Like the early morning dew

Give up your busy striving
To accomplish your selfish goals
Bow down before My altar and
I'll touch you with My coals

The corporate anointing
Will draw the souls to Me
When your love for one another
Is displayed in unity

Meet Me in the secret place
It's there I'll show you face to face
The things I have prepared for you

Hold on like Jacob, don't let go
And you'll receive the blessing
And My power you will know

Scripture

Then the man said, Let me go for it is daybreak. But Jacob replied, I will not let you go unless you bless me.
Genesis 32:26

How good and how pleasant it is, when brothers live together in unity. It is like the precious oil poured on the head, running down on the beard, running down on Aaron's beard, down upon the collar of his robes. It is as if the dew of Hermon were falling on Mt. Zion. Fore there the Lord bestows the blessing.
Psalm 133

Get Ready To Soar

Can you see the eagle up high
Gliding, soaring effortlessly through the sky
That is how the Lord wants you and I to soar

As the eagle is perched on his nest
So the Lord wants us to be at rest
The eagle is waiting and anticipating
For the wind to blow again
To lift him up and carry him

When we wait on the Lord
With thanksgiving, praising and singing
The Holy Ghost will come by
And lift out spirits way up high

Riding on the Joy of the Holy Ghost
Rejoicing to the uttermost
Being filled with His strength
Renewed within, fainting no more, learning to soar

Just like the One-hundred-and-twenty
In the upper room in Jerusalem
Were waiting, praying and anticipating this new thing
The Lord had promised He would bring

So again we are watching, waiting and anticipating
For the latter rain to pour and the wind to blow once more

If you are not born again, just call on Jesus' Name
And you too will be filled with the Father's Love
And your spirit will be soaring up above
On the wings of the heavenly Dove

 WALLI ANTONIE ZAMORANO

Scripture

*But they that wait upon the Lord shall renew their
strength They shall mount up with wings as eagles
they shall run and not be weary they shall walk
and not faint
Isaiah 40: 31*

*Who satisfieth thy mouth with good things so that
thy youth is renewed like the eagle's.
Psalm 103: 5*

*And suddenly there came a sound from heaven
as of a mighty rushing wind and it filled all the
house where they were sitting.
Acts 2:2*

Hear The Lion Roar

When you lift up your voices to the Lord
Worshipping Him in one accord
Then you can hear the Lion roar
And summon his mighty angels to war

When the high praises are in your mouth
And the two-edged sword is in your hand
Then you can hear the Lion roar
And deliverance will be seen in the land

When you shout for Joy and clap your hands
And worship before Him in holy dance
Then you can hear the Lion roar
The forces of darkness have lost once more

When the watchmen will not hold their peace
From sounding the alarm they will not cease
Then you can hear the Lion roar
And the King of Glory shall arise
As a mighty man of war

When the outpouring of His Spirit will begin
And the final harvest has come in
Then you can hear the Lion roar
His return will be even at the door

Scripture

Behold, the Lion of the Tribe of Judah, the
Root of David has prevailed.
Revelations 5:5

They shall walk after the Lord, he shall roar
like a lion, when he shall roar the children
shall tremble from the west.
Hosea 11:10

The Lord shall go forth, as a mighty man he shall
stir up jealousy like a man of war, he shall cry,
yea, roar; he shall prevail against the enemy.
Isaiah 42:13

I've Prepared The Way

I've prepared the way before you
Won't you come and enter in
The Blood of the Lamb
Will cleanse you from all sin

I've prepared the way before you
Won't you come and enter in
Through the Gates of Praise
In joyful song your voices raise

I've prepared the way before you
Won't you come and enter in
When the Oil of Joy you receive
All of your heaviness will leave

I've prepared the way before you
Won't you come and enter in
Come into the Holy Place
There I'll meet you face to face.

I've prepared the way before you
Won't you come and enter in
Come and kneel before My Throne
Bow down and worship Me alone

Scripture

To appoint unto them that mourn in Zion
to give unto them beauty for ashes, the oil
of Joy for mourning, the garment of praise
for the spirit of heaviness.
Isaiah 61:3

Enter his gates with thanksgiving and his
courts with praise, be thankful unto him
and bless his name.
Psalm 100

Let us therefore come boldly unto the throne
of Grace, that we may obtain mercy, and find
grace to help in time of need.
Hebrews 4:16

Joy Comes In The Morning

Are you weary today
Do you want to quit the good fight
Are you frustrated
Because nothing is going right

The Word of God tells us to rejoice
It is contrary to how we feel
Nevertheless it is very real
The only way out is with a shout

When you offer the sacrifice of Joy
Your head will be lifted high
Above the enemy's ploy
Wait on the Lord and you will see
New strength be given thee

One day when I was depressed
I didn't feel like getting dressed
When I looked in the mirror, I could hardly see
Through the swollen eyes, looking back at me

Then I heard a voice from within
It said, Self pity is a sin
The only way out of depression
Is the opposite confession
When you bring the sacrifice of Praise
Your countenance he will raise

The Word of God remains true
Even if it doesn't make sense to you
Weeping may last all night
But Joy comes in the morning light

Scripture

And now shall mine head be lifted up above
mine enemies round about me; therefore will
I offer in his tabernacle sacrifices of Joy; I
will sing, yea I will sing praises to the Lord.
Psalm 27:6

For His anger endureth but for a moment in his
favor is life; weeping may endure all night, but
Joy cometh in the morning.
Psalm 30:5

If I Were An Eagle

If I were an eagle
I would spread my wings and fly
Soaring passed the clouds way up high
Reaching out to touch the sky

Effortlessly rising
On the wings of the wind
Weightlessly gliding not bound
By any earthly thing

Higher and higher it is taking me
Smaller and smaller is what I see
Looking down from Heaven's canopy
My spirit is shouting victory

There is a change in the atmosphere
There is no room for fear way up here
A new sound is coming into my ear
As to Heaven's gate I am drawing near

The song of Heaven I now hear
A symphony I never heard before
A multitude of celestial voices
Blending into one accord

O what ecstasy there will be
For us to enjoy throughout eternity
O the glory waiting for you and me
When our blessed Savior we shall see

When we leave this earth some day
Casting off our temple made of clay
Soaring with the eagle
Up, up and away

 WALLI ANTONIE ZAMORANO

Scripture

*But they that wait upon the Lord, shall renew
their strength they shall mount up with wings
as eagles, they shall run, and not be weary, they
shall walk and not faint.*
Isaiah 40:31

*Who satisfieth thy mouth with good things,
so that thy youth this renewed as the eagles.*
Psalm 103:5

New Beginnings

A New Beginning is for all
Who will listen to His call

A New Beginning you can see
When you lift your eyes to Calvary
Jesus died for you, your spirit to renew
A New Beginning is for everyone
Who will accept what He has done

A New Beginning you will find
When you renew your mind

A New Beginning is assured
When from sickness you are cured
Jesus bore stripes on His back
So you and I will have no lack

A New Beginning will restore all
Adam had before the Fall
When he disobeyed God's command
From the garden he was banned

A New Beginning is what this life
Here on this earth is all about
When you experience this new birth
You will not miss out
You and I together
Will leave this planet with a shout

Scripture

*Jesus answered and said unto him; Verily, verily
I say unto you, except a man be born again, he
cannot see the kingdom of God.
John 3:3*

*And be not conformed to this world; but be ye
transformed by the renewing of your mind,
that ye may prove what is that good, and
acceptable, and perfect will of God.
Romans 12:2*

*He was wounded for our transgressions, He was
bruised for our iniquities, the chastisement of our
peace was upon him, and with His stripes we
are healed.
Isaiah 53:5*

Prepare

Prepare the way
Prepare the way for me
Cast up the highway for your King

Cleanse your heart
Cleanse it and let it be
Consecrated unto me

Turn away
Turn away from yesterday
Forsake all of your sin

Shut the door
Shut the door to before
Don't let temptation in

Give to me
Give to me your all
I'll answer when you call

Worship me
Worship me alone
Bow down at my Throne

Scripture

*Go through, go through the gates; prepare ye
the way of the people; cast up, cast up the
highway; gather out the stones; lift up a
standard for the people.*
Isaiah 62:10

*And a highway shall be there, and a way and
it shall be called the way of holiness; the unclean
shall not pass over it…*
Isaiah 35:8

Seedtime And Harvest

Have you heard
It is written in the Word
Whatever seed is sown
Will bring the harvest that is grown

From the beginning God made the decree
As long as heaven and earth shall be
Seedtime and harvest will remain
It is established in Jesus' Name

If a farmer wants a barn full of wheat
So his family has bread to eat
He must sow the best kernels of grain
For a plenteous harvest to gain

The Law of the Harvest will work for you
If you do what the Word tells you to
Give and it shall given unto you

All our deeds will be tested
Every man's works manifested
If they're done out of man's desire
They won't make it through the fire

They are wood, stubble and hay
Only the ashes will stay
This man will barely be saved

The works that are done
In obedience to God alone
Are gold, silver and precious stone

Tested in the fire they will remain
And a reward for that man gain

WALLI ANTONIE ZAMORANO

Scripture

*As long as the earth endures, Seedtime and
harvest, cold and heat, summer and winter,
day and night will never cease.*
Genesis 8:22

*Therefore all things whatsoever ye would that
man do to you, do ye even to them . For this
is the law and the prophets.*
Matthew 7:12

See The Lord

Can you see the Lord
Do you see Him walking on the water
Everything is possible with the Lord
He likes you and loves you even more

When you give Him your life
And love Him with all your might
He will show you his Grace
And will walk with you in every place

He will climb the mountain with you
And show you His mercy too
He will forgive your sin
And heal your wounds within

O how wonderful it is
When you are one of His
It is hard to understand
That our name is written
In the palm of His hand

It is difficult to comprehend
That the creator of this world
Says He is my friend
Will hold us in His arm
To keep us from all harm

Jesus Christ will be the King
Ruling over everything

Scripture

And he saw them toiling in rowing; as for the wind was contrary unto them; and about the fourth watch of the night he cometh unto them, walking upon the sea, and would have passed by them; But when they saw him walking upon the sea they supposed it had been a spirit, and cried out: For they all saw him, and were troubled. And immediately he talked with them, and said unto them, Be of good cheer it is I; be not afraid.
Mark 6:48-50

The Lord shall reign for ever and ever......
Exodus 15:18

The Beam

Father, please help me see
What has been blinding me
Help me to lay down my pride
And not insist that I am right

The only way to restore harmony
Is for me to go to Calvary
That is the only place
Where the Blood of Jesus
Can once again my sin erase

I must take down my wall of self-defense
And admit my own negligence
Lord, I have fallen short
There is nothing
That can support my attitude
I simply have been rude

All this time I didn't realize the beam
That was blinding my own eyes
Thank You for using my neighbor
To help me clearly see
What was inside of me

I cannot blame my nationality
Or even my own personality
You require, that I come up higher
And walk in love and humility

Lord, help me to remove the beam
Out of my own eye, so I can see
That I may be my neighbor's friend
And not his enemy

WALLI ANTONIE ZAMORANO

Scripture

And why beholdest thou the mote that is in
thy brother's eye, but considereth not the
beam that is in thine own eye?

Or how wilt thou say to thy brother;
Let me pull out the mote out of thine eye,
and, behold, a beam is in thine own eye.
Matthew 7:3,4

The Bleating Of The Sheep

Can you hear the bleating of the sheep
Can you hear the people weep
Green pastures they have not found
Dry and barren is the ground
There is no fresh water to quench their thirst
Only empty cisterns filled with dirt

Is there anyone who cares
And their heavy burden shares
Can you hear their cry and their hopeless sigh

I have good news for all the bleating sheep
There is someone, who will meet your every need
It is the Good Shepherd
He will leave the ninety-nine behind
And search until the one lost little lamb He'll find

He will restore your soul and He will make you whole
He will anoint you with fresh oil. No more need to toil

He is the living bread. He will keep your spirit fed
When you are thirsty and dry
He'll give you living water and you shall never die

In every storm and trial He will be your guide
He promised to stay forever by your side
He will comfort you and bring you safely through

Walli Antonie Zamorano

Scripture

Why abodest thou among the sheepfolds, to hear
the bleatings of the flocks? For the divisions
of Reuben there are great searching of heart.
Judges 5:16

The Lord is my Shepherd, I shall not want.
He maketh me to lie down in green pastures. He
leadeth me beside the still waters. He restoreth
my soul. He leadeth me in paths of righteousness
for His Name's sake. Thou preparest a table
before me in the presence of mine enemies; Thou
anointest my head with oil; my cup runneth over.
Psalm 23: 1-3,5

The Fear Of The Lord

Do you fear the Lord
Do you tremble at His Word

God loves him, who is contrite
Who is walking in the light
The one who will from evil depart
Is close to the Father's heart

To those who fear Him and stay away from strife
He promises a fountain of life
His Truth and Mercy He will extend
And bring our iniquity to an end

.

The Lord will reveal His secrets to those
Who have kept His covenant and drawn close
To His servants, the prophets, He will show
The things He wants only them to know

Strong confidence this "Fear of God" will bring
To those who stay in reverence before the King
To them who fear the Lord there is no lack
Not any good thing will He withhold
Even the angels are watching over us, we are told

We cannot lose
When the "Fear of the Lord" we choose
Our souls shall dwell at ease
Our children find a place of peace
We cry out in one accord

Father
Please teach us the Fear of the Lord

 WALLI ANTONIE ZAMORANO

Scripture

The angel of the Lord campeth about them that
fear Him, and delivereth them.
O, fear the Lord all His saints. There is no want
to them that fear him.
Psalm 34: 7,9

Come ye children, hearken unto me, and I will
teach you the fear of the Lord,
Psalm 34:11

The fear of the Lord tendeth to life; and he that hath
it shall remain satisfied. He shall not be visited with evil.
Proverbs 19:23

Time Out

Don't wait, until it is too late
Time is not standing still
Seasons come and seasons go
People running to and fro

Stop and think about your Maker
Your life is but a vapor
Here today and gone tomorrow
Time is a thing you cannot borrow

Time out! Is what I say. Take a break
Your eternal future is at stake
Get to know your Maker
Before you meet the undertaker

Now is the time to pray
In My presence stay
Call upon My Name
I am still the same
Yesterday, today and tomorrow
I'm the One to take your sorrow
And turn it into joy and gladness
Forsake this world's madness

Come into a solitary place So I can meet you face to face
Just believe and trust Me now
To the enemy you must never bow
He is a liar and a thief
His goal is to deceive
Be not alarmed, what life may bring
Be assured, I am in control of everything

 Walli Antonie Zamorano

Scripture

Jesus Christ the same yesterday, and today, and for ever.
Hebrews 13:8

The thief cometh not but for to steal, and to kill,
and to destroy, I am come that they might have
life and that they might have it more abundantly.
John 10:10

For God has not given us the spirit of fear but
of power, and of love and of a sound mind.
II Timothy 1:7

To Whom It May Concern

The gates of heaven will be shut forever
To those who sought Me never
Did I not make you in My image
My heart is broken over you
For all the things you do

You spend your day, pleasing your own way
You declare to others you meet
That you know Me. That is deceit
You lack the wisdom that is from above
You reject the Father's love

Where will it lead you
You must ask yourself that question
Not heaven but hell will be the destination
For all who pursue their own imagination

Listen to what I have to say
You must turn around and repent
And give your life to Jesus
My Son who I have sent

You cannot make it on your own
Only the blood of Jesus can atone
For the sins that separate you from My throne

If you decide to heed this call and forsake it all
I will write your name in My book
You will be cleansed from your sin
The angels will rejoice
That you finally made it in

 Walli Antonie Zamorano

Scripture

*He that believeth on the Son has everlasting life;
and he that believeth not the Son shall not see
life; but the wrath of God abideth on him.
John 3:36*

*For all have sinned, and come short of the
Glory of God.
Romans 3:23*

*For the wages of sin is death; but the free gift of
God is eternal life through Jesus Christ our Lord.
Romans 6:23*

Two Roads

There are two roads from which to choose
Rejoicing with Joy or singing the blues
Win or lose which is it for you

There is a road that is narrow and straight
The only pathway that ends at Heaven's gate

It leads up a hill called Calvary
Passes by an old rugged tree
Where Jesus died for you and me
Bearing our sins and iniquity

At the cross time stands still
There we surrender our will
We lay down sin's crushing load
Freely leaping up the narrow road

There is a road that is broad and wide
It is inviting and desirable to the eye
Remember the devil is a liar
He wants us all in the Lake of Fire

If you want to escape God's wrath
You must stay on the narrow path
It will take you to the pearly gate

Today is the Day of Salvation
Right now is the time to repent
Make heaven your destination
Take the narrow road, my Friend

Scripture

Enter ye in at the straight gate for wide is the gate
and broad is the way that leadeth to destruction
and many there be that go in thereat.

Because strait is the gate and narrow is the
way that which leadeth unto life and few there
be that find it.
Matthew 7:13. 14

Unity

Jesus wants us all to know
That the Father loves us as much
as He loves the Son.
It is this Love that will make us one

If we would only believe that this is true
There would be no more fighting
Over who is right and who is wrong
The bond of unity would be strong

Through the ages it has been the enemy's goal
To keep the body of Christ from becoming whole
Once we are of one mind and speak what we believe
Nothing shall be impossible to achieve

When we are joined in this kind of unity
It will be the greatest witness for all the world to see
They will finally comprehend why Jesus was sent
Those who don't know Him will believe
And the message of salvation into their hearts receive

Let us give Praise and turn from our selfish ways
We must have pure hearts and clean hands
And be holy as the Word commands
Let's tear down the wall that is looming tall
That is dividing us from one another
Let us love each other

WALLI ANTONIE ZAMORANO

Scripture

And the glory which thou gavest me, I have given them;
that we may be one, even as we are one.
John 17:22

Behold, how good and how pleasant it is for brethren
to dwell together in unity.
Psalm 133:1

Who shall ascend into the hill of the Lord? or who
shall stand in his holy place? He that hath clean hands,
and a pure heart, who hath not lifted up his soul
unto vanity nor has sworn deceitfully.
Psalm 24: 3,4

What Must I Do?

O Lord, what must I do, how can I express my love for you
You are the all-knowing God; You know what's in my heart
I feel like we're a million miles apart
Lord, please give me a new start

O Lord, what must I do, how can I express my love for you
You are the all-seeing God; You can see right into me
If there is any sin, please make me clean within

O Lord, what must I do, how can I express my Love for you
It seems that every day, I still want my own way
Lord, how long will it be, until Christ is formed in me

O Lord, what must I do, how can I express my love for you
You are the omnipotent God; You've created all things
Mighty miracles you have wrought
Yet You know my every thought

O Lord, what must I do, how can I express my love for you
Father, full of Mercy and Grace, once again I seek your face
Please help me today, that no hurtful thing I'll say
O Lord, what must I do, how can I express my love for you
You are the omnipresent God, there is no place where I can hide
Everything is wide open in your sight

Thank You Lord, for showing me today
That there is nothing I can do or say
For which forgiveness has not made a way
Your unconditional Love for me is here to stay

Scripture

*He that loveth not, knoweth not God, for God
is Love.
I John 4:9*

*Let your conversation be without covetousness;
and be content with such things as you have;
for he hath said, I will never leave thee nor forsake
thee.
Hebrews 13:5*

Love Never Fails

Satisfy us in the Morning
with your unfailing Love
that we may sing for Joy and
be glad all of our days.

Psalm 90:14

All This

With tender loving Mercy
I have called you
So you would become a child of Mine

With the blood of My Son
I have washed you
So you can leave your sins behind

With My Righteousness
I have clothed you
So you can come to My table and dine

With My Holy Spirit I have baptized you
So you can let your light shine

With My Joy I have filled you
So renewed strength you will find

With My Peace I have surrounded you
And comforted your troubled mind

With My Love I have embraced you
To receive the Oil and the Wine

ALL THIS
I have done for you, to let you know
I LOVE YOU SO

Scripture

The Lord hath appeared of old unto me saying,
Yea, I have loved you with an everlasting love,
therefore with loving-kindness I have drawn thee.
Jeremiah 31:3

Peace I leave with you, my peace I give unto
you; not as the world giveth, give I you. Let not
your heart be troubled, neither let it be afraid.
John 14:27

Amazing Love

Amazing Love, how can it be
The Son of God would die for me
He says, I am His
And He is mine

Amazing Love, how can it be
The King of Kings would die for me
He says, before He came
He knew my name

Amazing Love, how can it be
The creator of the Universe would die for me
He says, He took my sin
Now I belong to Him

O, Lord accept my Praise
With trembling lips I raise
O, how can it be
That You are in love with me

You said, when You died
You purchased yourself a Bride
To reign forever at Your side

O, Lord now I see my destiny
And why You died for me
I am your Bride to be
Hidden in Your Love for all eternity

Scripture

*I am my beloved's and my beloved is mine;
he feedeth among the lilies.
Song of Solomon 6:3*

*For ye are bought with a price therefore
glorify God in your body and in your spirit,
which are God's.
I Corinthians 6:20*

*He that hath the Bride is the bridegroom, but
the friend of the bridegroom, which standeth
and heareth him, rejoiceth greatly because of
the bridegroom's voice: this my Joy is therefore
fulfilled.
John 3:39*

A Cry For The Children

All around the world
A cry for the children can be heard
God's heart is close to all those
Who give their care to little children everywhere

Whosoever receives a little child
In my Name, receives me, but not me alone
Also the Father who sits on the Throne

Jesus took the little children in His arm
And said
You must protect them from all harm
If you want to enter the kingdom
You must become meek and mild
And humble yourselves like a little child

We must take heed and take care of those in need
Children are the precious seed
The harvest that we will some day reap
Daily we must lift our voice in prayer
For our own and children everywhere

Every child is special and precious to the Lord
His heart is grieved over every baby we abort
For each one of them, there was a destiny
O what a shame and what a loss for all humanity

Lord, forgive us for this plight
We cannot make it right
The only thing we can do
Is to plead for Mercy from you

Scripture

*And he took a child, and set him in the midst
of them: and when he had taken him in his
arms, he said unto them,
Whosoever shall receive one of such children
in my name, receiveth me; and whosoever
shall receive me, receiveth not me, but him
that sent me.*
Mark 9:36,37

WALLI ANTONIE ZAMORANO

Color It Red

You all know the story about the King
Who came from Glory
Who left Heaven for a short season
And came to earth for only one reason
His blood a ransom for our sins to shed
Color it red

To Rahab the two spies said
Bind in your window this scarlet thread
You and your household shall be spared
Because for us you cared
Color it red

It is the color of the rose of Sharon
Which the Father chose to crush for us
So we could be made whole In our spirit
Body and soul His Word is our daily bread
Color it red

God so loved the world
That He sent His only Son to earth
Born in a manger - a humble birth
To give everlasting life to those
Whom he freely chose
Color it red

Its Name is LOVE. It comes from God above
Take a look in the book and you will find the thread
From Genesis to Revelation
It shows the plan of His Salvation
LOVE is painted red

Scripture

*Behold when we come into the land, thou shalt
bind this line of scarlet thread in the window
which thou didst let us down by; and shall bring
thy father and thy mother and thy brethren, and
all thy father's house-hold, home unto thee.*
Joshua 2:18

*For God so loved the world that he gave his only
begotten Son, so that whosoever believeth in him
shall not perish but have everlasting life.*
John 3:16

God's Love

God's Love is the real treasure
Too big for anyone to measure
Love is not complete until it meets somebody's need
Love is always kind, the best in everyone to find
Love is never rude or in an ugly mood

God's Love is also called compassion
It gives, and gives so that someone else lives
God's Love is everlasting, it keeps on sending
His Mercy and His Grace down to the human race
It is an never ending stream shining like a flood light's beam

God's Love seeks restoration. It offers us eternal salvation
When you think about what really matters
While we are on this earth
And what outlasts everything of worth, it is the second birth
When Jesus shed His blood for you and me
God's Love was plain for all the world to see

He washes all our sins away. He brightens our darkest day
He brings assurance and peace, from our worries sweet release
He liberates us and sets us free, the beauty of God's Love to see

God is all of the above, for God is Love
Love sits upon a throne, He rules this universe alone
Love's government shall never end
Faith and Hope will cease. Love will outlast all of these

We need to ask ourselves this question
Do we love one another? Does our forgiveness cover Forgive me, Lord!
I am falling short

Scripture

*For God so loved the world, that He gave His
only begotten Son, that whosoever believeth in
him, should not perish, but have everlasting life.*
John 3:16

*Love suffereth long and is kind; love envies not;
love vaunts not itself, is not puffed up.
Does not behave itself unseemly, seeks not her
own, and is not easily provoked, thinks no evil.*
I Corinthians 13: 4-6

God So Loved

God so loved the world
That He gave His only Son
To save us from damnation
And grant us His Salvation

God so loved the world
That He gave His only Son
To save all who will call
From the curse of the Fall

God so loved the world
That He gave His only Son
To save all who will believe
And His free gift receive

God so loved the world
That He gave His only Son
To save all who will confess
His Name and proclaim
That Jesus rose again

God so loved the world
That He gave His only Son
To save YOU from your sin
When YOU call out to Him

Scripture

*For God so loved the world that He gave His only
begotten Son, that whosoever believeth in Him
should not perish, but have everlasting life.*
John 3:16

*But God commendeth his love toward us, In that,
while we were yet sinners, Christ died for us.*
Romans 5:8

I Love You

You are the one I love
I've been watching you from above
Let me dry your tears
Let me take away your fears
Do you remember when we first met
When you gave me your heart
And swore, that nothing could keep us apart
O, how I long to be your friend
I want our relationship to mend

Did you not recognize the devil's clever lies
My Word is true, I've never forsaken you

Or has your love for Me grown cold
Because of something somebody told
Is it because of an offense

Don't let the devil have his way
He doesn't want you to pray
Discouragement he wants to bring
He doesn't want anyone to sing

Here is the way out: Forgiveness is the key
I did it for you on Calvary
Love one another, as I have loved you
Is that so hard to do

Yes, you'll have to lay down your pride
To make things right
Believe me, what I said is true
I will never stop loving You

Scripture

*A new commandment give I unto you, that ye love
one another; as I have loved you, that ye also love
one another.*
John 13:34

*Behold, I stand at the door and knock, if any man
hear my voice and open the door, I will come in to
him and will sup with him, and he with me.*
Revelation 4:20

*Greater Love has no man than this, that a man
lay down his life for his friend.*
John 15:13

 WALLI ANTONIE ZAMORANO

I See You

I see you when you're happy
I see you when you're sad
I see you when you're angry
I see you when you're glad
You're always in My sight
Morning, noon and night
I've made you for My pleasure
You are My delight

I see you when you're sleeping
I see you when you're awake
I see you when you're weeping
Also in a joyful state
You are very special
You are one of a kind
Before I ever formed you
I had your picture in My mind

I see you when you're friendly
I see you when you're rude
I see you when you're lovely or have an attitude
You are worth more than the sparrow
There are many of them in the fold

When I made you, My Precious
I threw away the mold.
I see you when you praise me
I see you when you pout
I see when you have faith
I see when you have doubt

Your praise is a sweet fragrance
It rises up to My throne
Let Me assure you of My love for you
even if you sometimes fail in what you do

Scripture

*Are not two sparrows sold for a farthing and one of
them shall not fall to the ground without your father.
Fear ye not therefore, you are of more value than
many sparrows.*
Matthew 10:29,31

*O Lord, thou hast searched me and thou hast known
me. Thou knowest mine down sitting and mine
uprising, thou understandest my thoughts afar off.
Thou compassest my path and my lying down and
art acquainted with all my ways.*
Psalm 139

I Will Always Love You

Even though you are old and your hair is grey
Your faith is still strong and you have not lost the way
Many trials and tests you have come through
I want you to know, I have not forgotten you

All those who wait on me, like eagles they shall be
Their strength I will renew, many exploits they shall do
Its in the place of prayer, my plans with you I'll share
That's when you'll discover, I've been your only Lover

Love is not something you feel
Only Love - that gives itself - is real
Faith and Hope will pass away
My Love for you is here to stay
From the place of my habitation

I look down on every nation
To seek the one who fears my name
Who knows my Son and why he came

You've been faithful throughout the years
Through happy times and times of tears
You may be old
But my love for you has not grown cold

The love that I gave will come back multiplied
It is the law of the harvest, I have myself applied
My Son willingly died, so He could have a bride

Get ready! Time is running out
All who Love me will hear the shout
Watch and pray
Nobody knows the day nor the hour
When I come in my Power

Scripture

*Beloved, let us love one another for love is of God; and
every one that loveth is born of God and knoweth God.
He that loveth not, knoweth not God, for God is Love.*

*In this was manifested the Love of God toward us,
because that God sent his only begotten Son into the
world, that we might live through him.*

*Herein is love, not that we loved God but that he loved
us and sent his Son to be the propitiation for our sins.
Beloved, if God so loved us, we ought also to love oneanother.*
I John 4: 7-11

I Will Never Abandon You

Do not fear, when the storms are drawing near
Take refuge under My wing. I'll keep you safe this very hour
I am your strong tower. I'll give you overcoming power
I am your security. Come, hide yourself in Me
Until this calamity is over past and there is calm at last

Seek Me early and draw near
My still small voice you will hear
I'll tell you of My love for you
And instruct you in what to do
In the cleft of the rock you must stay
Until the storm clouds have gone away

When you leave the cares of this world behind
In My presence true fulfillment you will find
Come sit at My table and eat
It is there where we will meet
The bread, I have to give
Will impart new sustenance to live
O, what a glorious union
When we are joined in holy communion
I'll give you Joy and Peace, all anxiety will cease

Sing to Me a joyful song. It will make you strong
Even if the trouble wants to stay, praise Me anyway
I am your light and your salvation. Lord over every situation
I am your hiding place
Through your songs of Praise the enemy you will chase
He will flee from you in seven ways
My promise is true, I will never, never abandon you
This is how it's going to be
Me loving you and you loving Me
Throughout all eternity

Scripture

*The Lord is my light and my salvation, whom shall
I fear? the Lord is the strength of my life, of whom
shall I be afraid?
For in the time of trouble he shall hide me in his
pavilion; in the secret of his tabernacle shall he
hide me; he shall set me up upon a rock.
Psalm 27: 1,5*

*Thou art my hiding place; thou shalt preserve
me from trouble; thou shalt compass me about
with songs of deliverance.
Psalm 32: 7*

Love As Long As You Can

Sing as long as you can
Sing as long as you may
The hour may come
When the melody is gone
And silence lasts all day

Dance as long as you can
Dance as long as you may
The hour may comes
When the music stops to play

Rejoice as long as you can
Rejoice as long as you may
The hour may come
When the enemy comes
And steals your joy away

Pray as long as you can
Pray as long as you may
The hour may come
When doubt comes in to stay

Love as long as you can
Love as long as you may
The hour will come
When you stand at the grave
And there is nothing left to say

Love as long as you can
Love as long as you may

Scripture

Now also when I am old and grey headed, O God
forsake me not; until I have shewed thy strength
unto this generation, and thy power to everyone
that is to come.
Psalm 71:18

I will sing a new song unto thee, O God; upon
a psaltery and on an instrument of ten strings
will I sing praises to you.
Psalm 144:9

Love Is Reaching Out

Love one another, just as I have loved you
That's what Jesus said to do
Love is the answer to everything
Peace and Joy it is sure to bring
Out of Love the Father sent the Son
To give His life for everyone

Through His death He brought Salvation
To rescue us from eternal damnation
When we ask Him into our heart
This Love He will impart

Now this Love in you and me will help us to be
His instruments to reach out to all who are without

This Love of God in us cannot fail
Over every trial and test it will prevail
It will comfort all who are sad
And make the weary glad
It will never cease, it will bring Peace
It will defeat every foe, it will conquer every woe

Before the world began, Love made the demand
To provide a second chance to all who will come
Through the sacrifice of His Son

The circle will be unbroken
Just as the prophets have spoken
This Love of God in every woman, child and man
Will take us back to heaven where it all began

Love has provided the way, Love is here to stay
Love will never pass away
Love is reaching out to you today

Scripture

For God so loved the world that He gave His only
begotten Son that whosoever believeth on Him
shall not die but shall have everlasting Life.
John 3:16

This is my commandment, that ye love one another,
as I have loved you.
John 15:12

And now abideth Faith, Hope and Love these three,
but the greatest of these is LOVE.
I Corinthians 13:13

Love Never Fails

My heart is filled with gratitude
A thousand thanks won't be enough
To thank the Father for His Love

Love had to take the ultimate test
When God offered His very best
When His Son hung on that tree
His blood was shed for you and me

His blood was not like yours or mine
His blood was divine
Eternal life flowed in His veins
Pure and holy, free from sin's stains

Love had to be crucified
For sinful man to be justified
When they drove in the nails
He forgave them, for Love never fails

Everyone, who calls on His Name
He loves the same
Jew or Gentile, black or white
They all are precious in His sight

When we ask Him to come into our hearts
That's when the miracle starts
His Life, His light, and His Love
Has come down from above
To dwell in you and me for all eternity

Scripture

*For God so loved the world, that He gave His only
begotten Son, that, whosoever believeth in Him
shall not perish, but have everlasting life.*
John 3:16

*And the Spirit and the Bride say come. And let
him that heareth say, Come. And let him that is
athirst come and whosoever will, let him take the
water of life freely.*
Revelation 22:17

My First Love

Jesus, you are my First Love now
Humble at your feet I bow
You came down from the Father above
And laid down your life for Love

When I was forsaken and all alone
You came down from Your throne
You found me and brought peace
From my misery sweet release

Now I can clearly see
Your love came in and lifted me
Your precious blood has set me free
When You poured it out on Calvary

There is no greater Love I know
And that's the reason why I love You so
Please Lord, take my life and let it be
My love song to You for all eternity

Scripture

*Nevertheless I have somewhat against you, because
thou hast left thy first love.*
Revelation 2:4

*And they sang a new song, saying, thou art worthy
to take the book, and to open the seals thereof for
thou wast slain, and redeemed us to God by thy blood
out of every kindred, and tongue and nation.*
Revelation 5:9

No Need To Be Afraid

You don't have to be afraid
When the earth begins to shake
If a strong foundation you have laid
You don't have to be afraid

You don't need to be alarmed
You will not be harmed
If with the blood of Jesus you are armed
You don't need to be alarmed

You do not need to fear
You won't have to shed a tear
When you resist the devil and draw near
You do not need to fear

You can stay in perfect Peace
From all your worries cease
My Word will keep your mind at ease
You can stay in perfect Peace

You can even walk in Joy
My strength to you it will employ
The enemy's strongholds to destroy
You can even walk in Joy

You must always walk in Love
Coming down from above
Being filled with the Spirit
The gentle Dove
You must always walk in Love

Scripture

*I press toward the mark for the prize of the high
calling of God in Christ Jesus.*
Philippians 3:14

*The Lord is my rock, and my fortress and
my deliverer, my God, my strength, in whom
I will trust; my buckler, and the horn of my
Salvation, and my high tower.*
Psalm 18:2

*The earth shook and trembled; the foundations
also of the hills moved and were shaken, because
he was wroth.*
Psalm 18:7

Return To Me

Return, return, return to me
Hear my call both great and small
I love you all
Have you forgotten Me

Do you remember the day
When you first came to Me
The day I set you free
And washed your sins away

I have not changed My mind
still Mercy you can find
My arms are opened wide
To comfort you in your lonely night

Return, return, I am waiting at the cross
Don't pass by again
I will not always strive with man

Don't slip away and think
There'll be another day
That day may never come
And you will be left behind
Now is the time to change your mind

Father is waiting to welcome you back
In His house there is no lack
So, what do you say
Will you come today

Scripture

Return ye backsliding children, and I will heal
your backslidings, Behold, we come unto thee;
for thou art the Lord our God.
Jeremiah 3:22

And the Lord said, My Spirit shall not always
strive with man, for that he also is flesh: yet
his days shall be an hundred and twenty years.
Genesis 6:3

And he arose and came to his Father. But
when he was yet a great way off, his father
saw him and had compassion, and ran, and
fell on his neck and kissed him.
Luke 15:20

Walli Antonie Zamorano

So Great Love

O, what great Love
came down from the Father above
when He sent His only Son to Calvary
To make an atonement for humanity

Jesus was willing to die for you and I
There is no greater Love than His
There is no greater Love than this
That a man lay down his life for his friends

The greatness of this Love we cannot measure
It is more valuable than any earthly treasure
Like a little child we must come to Him
With a trusting heart and humble spirit within

Looking to the Joy set before Him
He was willing the sacrifice to bring
He endured the cross despising the shame
So we could become worthy of His Name

Forever grateful I will be
For His great Love poured out for me
When He carried the cross to Calvary
When He took my place up on that tree

This free gift we must not neglect
This offer we cannot reject
Salvation He has extended to all
Who will listen to His call

Scripture

*For God so loved the world, that He gave His only
begotten Son, that whosoever believeth in Him shall
not perish, but have everlasting life.*
John 3:16

*Looking unto Jesus the author and finisher of our
faith who for the joy that was set before him endured
the cross, despising the shame, and is set down at the
right hand of the throne of God.*
Hebrews 12:2

WALLI ANTONIE ZAMORANO

The Fire Of His Love

We must have revival, Lord, the people say, we are bored
Its too hard to fast and pray, can't you do something anyway

He'll come down from above with the Fire of His love
Who can abide in that day, when He comes
To take our filthiness away

He will suddenly appear. Who shall keep standing
Who is able to draw near
Like a refiner and a purifier, He'll kindle in us a holy fire

From time to time He'll turn the furnace higher
Until the dross is removed and the gold and silver glow
All our impurities must go
Our garments must be white as snow

It is God's desire for all His saints to be on fire
Fervent in spirit serving Him
The flame of their First Love burning bright within

In this final hour, we all need to move in His power
We must be willing vessels, yielded totally to Him
So we can bring the final harvest in

Let us draw near
And worship the Lord with reverence and with godly fear
He wants us to come up higher
Remember
OUR GOD IS A CONSUMING FIRE

Scripture

Behold, I will send my messenger, and he will
prepare the way before me; and the Lord whom
ye seek, shall suddenly come to his temple, even
the messenger of the covenant, whom ye delight
in; behold, he shall come saith the Lord of hosts.

But who may abide in the day of His coming?
and who shall stand when He appeareth? For
he is like a refiner's fire, and like fuller's soap.
And He shall sit as a refiner and purifier of
silver, and he shall purify the sons of Levi,
and purge them as gold and silver, that they may
offer unto the Lord an offering in righteousness.
Malachi 3:1-3

WALLI ANTONIE ZAMORANO

The River Of God's Love

Like a mighty river from above
Flows the Father's Love
He gave His Son to die for you
What more could he do

So His instructions would be heard
He gave to us His Word
The Holy Scripture is the name
Or Holy Bible, its the same
From Genesis to Revelation
It tells the story of God's Salvation

How it all began
When God first made man
How Adam disobeyed and from the tree
That was forbidden ate

Sin entered in, fellowship was lost
Separation from God the cost

God's Love did not cease
It found a new release
When the fullness of time had come
He sent His only begotten Son
To shed his precious blood
For us the cleansing flood

The Father wants you to know
You can still get into its flow
When you ask Jesus in
Another river will begin
The Love of God in you and me
For all the world to see

Scripture

*For God so loved the world, that He gave His
only begotten Son, that whosoever believeth in Him
should not perish, but have everlasting life.*
John 3:16

*So God created man in His own image, in the
image of God created He him; male and female
created He them.*
Genesis: 1:27

*But of the tree of the knowledge of good and evil,
thou shalt not eat of it; for in the day that thou eatest
thereof thou shalt surely die.*
Genesis 2:18

The Second Birth

When God made man in His own image
He breathed His Spirit into him
So through this holy union
God and man would be in close communion
To test man's loyalty, God set man's spirit free
To choose his own destiny

We all know what Adam and Eve did
When in the bushes they hid
When they disobeyed and ate,
They found out it was too late
When Adam fell from Grace
So did the whole human race

O, Glory and Thanksgiving to the Almighty
The God of Mercy and Grace
Who found a substitute to take our place
God sent His only begotten Son
Who by shedding his innocent blood
The victory over Satan won
So fellowship between God and man
Could be restored again to how it all began

It is a mystery to us, how it could be
When we ask Jesus into our heart
We will have a brand new start
His Spirit who from Adam He withdrew
Comes back into our hearts to make us new
Let this be that special day
Ask Jesus into your heart to stay

Scripture

*Jesus answered and said unto him, Verily, verily,
I say unto thee, Except a man be born again he
cannot see the kingdom of God.*
John 3:3

Marvel not that I say, You must be born again.
John 3:7

*And almost all things are by the law purged with
blood and without shedding of blood is no remission.*
Hebrews 9:22

Being Born Again

Jesus answered and said unto
him, Verily, verily, I say unto thee,
Except a man be born again, he
cannot see the kingdom of God.

John 3:3

Come Up Higher

Come up higher! Can you hear Him calling you
All that wait upon the Lord, you see
Like eagles they shall be
They shall spread their wings
And soar high above all earthly things

Their spirits will break free
From their temples made of clay
Their soul will rejoice in Him
When they begin to sing

Just as the eagles their feathers molt
And they get a brand new coat
So also our youth shall be renewed
As He satisfies our mouth with His good food

As the mother eagle spreads her feathers
To protect her babies from the weather
So the Almighty will cover us
When under His wings we trust

When the eaglet begins to fly
Soaring helplessly through the stormy sky
And the mother hears its frightened call
She spreads her wings underneath to stop its fall

Can you see, what the Father is telling you and me
When in our walk with Him we stumble and fall
He hears us when we call
He picks us up and we are safe from all harm
Within His everlasting arms

 WALLI ANTONIE ZAMORANO

Scripture

*He shall cover thee with his feathers, and under
his wings shalt thou trust; his truth shall be thy
shield and buckler.*
Psalm 91:4

*But they that wait upon the Lord, shall renew
their strength; they shall mount up with wings
as eagles; they shall run, and not be weary; and
they shall walk, and not faint.*
Isaiah 40:31

*Who satisfieth thy mouth with good things;
so that thy youth is renewed like the eagle's.*
Psalm 103:5

Death Where Is Your Sting?

O, death where is your sting
Hallelujah, let your praises ring
For those who have salvation
Death is merely graduation
Jesus took away the key
And stripped Satan of all authority
We are forgiven for our sin
Destined to reign forever with our King

The angels will accompany us
When we are going home
No more on this earth to roam
As the gate of Pearl swings open wide
Another angel will escort us inside
O, what splendor, O, what brilliant light
Is shining from the throne so bright
Like an emerald rainbow it appears

A multitude too numerous to count
Are standing all around
They begin to sing a new song
Worthy is the Lamb who was slain
And came to life again

Jesus shed His blood to bring salvation
To every kindred, tongue, and nation
When you give your life to Him
He'll wash away your sin
And when your time here on earth is done
Your eternal life in heaven has just begun

 WALLI ANTONIE ZAMORANO

Scripture

*I am he that liveth, and was dead; and, behold,
I am alive for evermore, Amen; and have the
keys of hell and of death.
Revelation 1:18*

*And he that sat was to look upon as a jasper and a
sardine stone: and there was a rainbow round about
the throne, in sight like unto an emerald.
Revelation 4:3*

*And the twelve gates were twelve pearls; every
several gate was of one pearl; and the street of the
city was pure gold, as it were transparent glass.
Revelation 21:21*

Don't Be Left Behind

Seek and you shall find
Don't be left behind
Do you know the Savior
Or do you think what counts
Is your good behavior

Your own goodness cannot save you
You must be born anew
We all have a spirit, a body and a soul
It is the spirit that must be made whole

When Adam and Eve sinned
God withdrew His Spirit
That had bonded them together
They were banned from the Garden forever
To redeem mankind from the Fall
God made a new way for us all

In His Mercy and His Grace
God sent His Son to take our place
His death provided the way of Salvation
For every man and every nation

Make haste! There is no time to waste
We do not know when, the Lord will descend
When that day is here, it will be too late
And you have sealed your fate

Today Salvation you can still find
Don't be left behind

 Walli Antonie Zamorano

Scripture

*That if thou confess with thy mouth the Lord Jesus
and shalt believe in thine heart that God hath raised
him from the dead, thou shalt be saved.
For with the heart man believeth unto righteousness
and with the mouth confession is made unto Salvation.*
Romans 10:9,10

*For whosoever shall call upon the Name of the Lord
shall be saved.*
Romans 10:13

God Inside

God is near, to all who hold Him dear
Who give Him their devotion
Who are a solid rock in the roaring ocean
Who are anchored in the Word of God
Not in their emotion

He will be their hiding place
And wipe the tears from their face
He will be their refuge and strength
A very present help in trouble

He will be their strong tower
In their darkest hour
When they put their trust in Him
Deliverance He will bring
And Songs of Praise to God they'll sing

Yes, this God, who created all
Made himself so small
That He can fit into our heart
Never again to depart

Let me briefly tell you how
You too can be that close to Him right now
All you have to do, is call upon His Name
His blood will cleanse you from all sin
He'll send His Holy Spirit within
And you'll be born again

     WALLI ANTONIE ZAMORANO

Scripture

Thou art my hiding place; thou shalt preserve me from trouble; thou shalt compass me about with songs of deliverance. Selah
Psalm 32:7

He only is my rock and my salvation: he is my defense; I shall not be moved.
In God is my salvation and my glory; the rock of my strength, and my refuge, is in God.
Psalm 62: 6,7

He Is Risen

The tomb is empty, come and see
There's an empty cross on a hill called Calvary
Mary and the other women came early in the day
They saw that the stone was rolled away
And Jesus wasn't there

The angels declared
Why do you seek the living among the dead
He has risen as he has said
Then they remembered Jesus' words
They returned to the eleven
And told, what they had seen and heard

Their tears were wiped away. This was Resurrection Day
Everything their Master had told them about
And what they knew, had now come true

Now, we have a reason to shout! HE IS RISEN
He took the keys from the enemy
Death where is your sting? Grave where is your victory

The only way you will be left out is if you doubt
It would be a terrible shame
And you would only have yourself to blame

So, join the redeemed of all the ages
Who couldn't pay their own wages
Who have trusted in the One
Who purchased our Salvation
And delivered us from eternal damnation

WALLI ANTONIE ZAMORANO

Scripture

*And it came to pass, as they were much perplexed,
there about, behold, two men stood by them in
shining garments;*

*And as they were afraid, and bowed down their
faces to the earth, they said unto them. Why seek ye
the living among the dead?*

*He is not here, but is risen; remember how he spake
unto you when he was yet in Galilee;*

*Saying, the Son of man must be delivered into the
hands of sinful men, and be crucified, and the third
day shall rise again.*
Luke 24: 4-7

My Kingdom In You

You must decide
If you will let My Kingdom come inside
When you ask Me to come into your heart
And repent of your sin
I'll forgive you and My Spirit will come in

Just as I did for Adam and Eve in the Garden
I am giving you the choice to obey My voice
I will speak inside of you
And let you know what you should do

Let my fire purify your desire
So your worship may be pure
And your confession sure

You'll become My ambassador on earth
To let others know about the second birth
Make the message clear
So that everyone will hear
That the kingdom of God is near

Testify and tell them what I did for you
When they profess Jesus Christ as their Lord
My Spirit will come aboard

Take my Word and run
A quick work must be done
Many more souls have yet to be won
To the Glory of my Son

 Walli Antonie Zamorano

Scripture

Neither shall they say, Lo here! or, lo there! For behold the kingdom of God is within you.
Luke 17:21

Jesus answered and said unto him, Verily, Verily, you must be born again
John 3:3

And he has raised us up together and made us sit together in heavenly places in Christ Jesus.
Ephesians 2:6

Salvation Has Come

Hear! Hear, lend me your ear
Both Gentile and Jew
I have Good News for you
Yeshua has come, God's only begotten Son
Just as the prophets had cried
He came and lived and died
He rose from the grave, He is alive

Just as it is written; He was smitten
They put a crown of thorns on him
And said that he was king
Then they nailed Him to a tree
The devil looking on with glee
He didn't know when Jesus was crucified
The way to salvation He would provide

When the devil thought He was dead
Jesus appeared before him instead
And took away the keys
And stripped him of all authority

Now all who call on Jesus' Name
Jew or Gentile just the same shall be saved
In the Word it is written
This is my covenant with them

When the fullness of the Gentiles has come in
I will take away their sin
All Israel shall be saved

The veil shall be lifted from their eyes
No longer to believe the devil's lies
Salvation has come for everyone

 WALLI ANTONIE ZAMORANO

Scripture

*For God so loved the world, that he gave his only
begotten Son, that whosoever believeth in him shall
not perish but have everlasting life.*
John 3:16

*For I would not that ye should be ignorant of this
mystery, lest ye should be wise in your own conceits;
that blindness in part has happened to Israel, until the
fullness of the Gentiles has come in.*

*And so all Israel shall be saved; as it is written, there
shall come out of Zion the deliverer and shall turn away
ungodliness from Jacob.*
Romans 11:25,26

So Great Salvation

He shed His blood for you and for me
Two-thousand years ago on a hill called Calvary
To save us from damnation
To purchase our salvation

He came to earth through humble birth
You all know the story of the angels in Glory
Announcing the Good News of God's plan
Known to the Father before the world began

The life is in the blood alone
Not in the flesh, nor in the bone
The mystery is this
When we ask Jesus into our lives to stay
His blood washes all our sins away
The kingdom of God has come into our heart
We are born again with a brand new start

The real purpose for our lives we'll find
When we are renewed within our mind
We must walk by faith and not by sight
Meditating in the Word both day and night
Then we'll be changed from glory to glory

His blood has never lost its power
Like a gentle rain and a refreshing shower
He sprinkles it on every nation
To bring the Good News of
'So great a Salvation'

 WALLI ANTONIE ZAMORANO

Scripture

*And suddenly there was with the angel a
multitude of the heavenly host praising God,
and saying, Glory to God in the highest and
on earth peace; good will toward men.*
Luke 2:13

*But we all, with open face beholding as in a glass
the Glory of the Lord, are changed into the
same image from Glory to Glory, even as by the
Spirit of the Lord.*
II Corinthians 3:18

*How shall we escape, if we neglect so Great Salvation,
which at first began to be spoken by the Lord and was
confirmed unto us by them that heard him.*
Hebrews 2:3

The Answer

There are questions
We all ask. Where did I come from
Why am I here and where am I going

To the Praise of His Glory we were created
God's Son came to this earth for one reason
To reverse Adam's treason

Before the world began
God already made a plan
How he would save lost man
He would give His Son
To die for the sins of everyone
His blood alone can for our sins atone
God's will for us here on earth
Is to have a second birth

When we confess with our mouth
That Jesus is Lord
He'll come in, and forgive us our sin

O, how wonderful it is
When you are one of His
What God expects us to do, is to stay true
And do what the Word tells us to do

Dear Friend, maybe now you will understand
My never ending concern for your life
It is because I know, that Jesus loves you so
Don't listen to man's suggestions

Only the Bible has the answer to our questions

 WALLI ANTONIE ZAMORANO

Scripture

That if thou with thy mouth confess the Lord Jesus,
and shalt believe in thine heart that God hath raised
him from the dead, thou shalt be saved.
For with the heart man believeth unto righteousness
and with mouth confession is made unto salvation.
Romans 10: 9,10

For God so loved the world that he gave his only
begotten Son, so that whosoever believeth on
him, shall not perish but have life everlasting.
John 3:16

The Choice

Have you met Him? He is the great King
Do you remember the crown He wore
Do you remember the stripes He bore
He shall rule the world to come
He is no other than God's only Son

With Justice and Grace He has taken His place
He is the only one, who qualified
To sit in judgment and divide
The nations from one another
Some to His right to be with Him forever
And some to the left, to see the Kingdom never

The Father has made the decree.
That the One who came to atone
To be the Judge and take His seat
on the Great White Throne

The day the door will be shut is drawing near
This is what nobody wants to hear
They just want someone to tickle their ear
Be not deceived in this hour
turn to the One who has the power

You must make your decision while you live
don't wait another day
JESUS is the Only Way
Rejoice and make Jesus your choice

Scripture

*How God anointed Jesus of Nazareth with the
Holy Ghost and with power; who went about
doing good and healing all that were oppressed
of the devil, for God was with him.*
Acts 10:38

*When the Son of man shall come in his glory
and all the holy angels with him, then shall he
sit upon the throne of his glory.*

*And before him shall be gathered all nations;
and he shall separate them one from another as
a shepherd divideth his sheep from the goats.*
Matthew 25:31,32

The Invitation

I am extending the invitation
To every kindred and every nation
Come on in and let the wedding feast begin Hearken unto my call
Both great and small may enter the festive hall
If you are late you are left outside the gate

As you have heard, in the beginning was the Word
The Word came to earth through a virgin birth
Jesus is His Name, He dwelt among you for a season
For the world's sin to atone His reason

If you are born again and cleansed from your sin
And my Holy Spirit lives within then you qualify
To meet Jesus in the sky

You'll hear a trumpet blast, my archangel will shout
You'll be one in that crowd going up into the cloud
The gates will be open wide
You'll see my Son, sitting at my side

The table will be spread.
You'll dine on Heaven's bread
Angels will bow before my Throne
Singing, Holy, Holy, Holy,
Worship Him alone

Scripture

*Then said he to his servants, The wedding is ready,
but they that were bidden were not worthy.*

*Go ye therefore into the highways, and as many
as ye shall find, bid to the marriage.*
Matthew 22: 8,9

*Jesus answered and said unto him; Verily, verily,
I say unto thee; Except a man be born again, he
cannot see the kingdom of God.*
John 3:3

*Who has delivered us from the power of darkness and
has translated us into the kingdom of his dear Son.*
Colossians 1:13

The Journey

When your journey on the road of life began
The Lord already had a plan
His plan is for good and not for evil
To give you hope, not just to cope
God's road leads to eternal life
the ultimate destination
The entrance to this path is our salvation

Everyone has to choose just like you
If he wants to make it through
God is not a respecter of persons
He treats everyone the same

When you have made the choice
To listen to God's voice
And accepted His invitation
And chose the way to Salvation

You will find the road is narrow
And not as easy as some have said
The difference is, you are not alone
The Holy Spirit will be your friend
He'll stick with you until the end
Heaven's gate will be opened wide
As the angels lead you safe inside

Scripture

For whosoever shall call on the Name of the
Lord, shall be saved.
Romans 10:13

For I know the thoughts that I think toward
you, saith the Lord, thoughts of peace and not
of evil, to give you an expected end.
Jeremiah 29:11

Because straight is the gate, and narrow is the way,
which leadeth to life, and few there be that find it.
Matthew 7:14

The Lamb And The Dove

A lamb is gentle, helpless and meek
Submissive and willing to do
whatever the shepherd tells him to

Wasn't that also Jesus' disposition
Who came by His own volition
He shed His innocent Blood on Calvary's tree
To become the substitute Lamb for you and me

When John the Baptist saw Jesus come
He knew that Jesus was God's Son
He cried, "Behold the Lamb of God
Which taketh away the sin of the world

Then a voice from Heaven was heard
This is my beloved Son
In whom I am well pleased
The Father in Heaven was satisfied
Because He knew when Jesus died
Many would be justified

Our sacrificed Lamb He has become
Just as a sheep before his shearers is dumb
He willingly endured the cross
Despising the shame
Looking to the Joy set before
When He will welcome us at Heaven's door

When we are born from above and walk in Love
We too become a resting place for the Dove

 WALLI ANTONIE ZAMORANO

Scripture

And lo a voice from heaven, saying, This is
my beloved Son in whom I am well pleased.
Matthew 3:17

The next day John seeth Jesus coming to him,
and saith, Behold the Lamb of God, which
taketh away the sin of the world.
John 1:29

He shall see of the travail of his soul, and shall
be satisfied; by his knowledge shall my righteous
servant justify many; for he shall bear their
iniquities.
Isaiah 53:11

The Master Potter

God says
He is the potter, we are the clay
He made each one of us in a very special way
You are one of a kind, no duplicate can anyone find

Of all the millions that have come and gone
He made you uniquely His own
How can it be, such infinite variety
The Master Potter takes great care
He fixes the vessels that need repair
He watches with great patience
Over His own creations

When our vessels have been marred
Or the clay has become hard
He knows just what to do
He puts us back on the wheel and starts anew
He shapes and molds us once again
Until we are pliable in His loving hand

One more thing He does require
We must go through the fire
The time in the oven may vary
But it is necessary
When you are finally finished
And your pain has diminished

He will look into the glaze
And see the reflection of His face
He is the Master Potter
You cry out to Him. Here I am! Use me
I am ready to fulfill my destiny

 WALLI ANTONIE ZAMORANO

Scripture

*But now O Lord, thou art our father; we are the
clay, and thou our potter; and we all are the work
of your hand.*
Isaiah 64:8

*And the vessel that he made of clay was marred
in the hand of the potter; so he made it again
another vessel, as seemed good, to the potter to
make it.*
Jeremiah 18:4

The Miracle Of Being Born Again

Dear Lord Jesus, please help me to explain
To write down and make plain
The miracle of being born again

When His salvation you will find
It seems as if you had been blind
And a veil had covered your mind
And someone came and set you free
Ripped off the veil and now you see

O Lord, with what can I compare
The miracle that will occur
When the Good News we will share
And Your Word decree and declare

It is like a bird escaping a snare
It's like not having a single care
It's like you are floating on air
Suddenly having a burning desire
To tell the Good News everywhere

At the moment that Jesus comes in
Your brand new life will now begin
He forgives all of your ugly sin
And sends the Holy Spirit in

You will know, that you know
Something happened deep within
You will know that you know
The miracle of being born again

 WALLI ANTONIE ZAMORANO

Scripture

Jesus answered and said unto him, Verily,
Verily I say unto thee, except a man be born
again, he cannot see the kingdom of God.
John, 3:3

Verily, verily I say unto thee, except a man
be born of water and of the Spirit he cannot
enter the kingdom of God.
That which is born of flesh is flesh
And that which is born of the Spirit is spirit.

Marvel not that I said unto thee, you must
be born again.
John 3: 5- 7

The Most Important Thing

Are you ready
To stand before the throne

God does not let us know
When we'll be going home

We must cherish every day
And follow in His way

He alone knows
The time we have here on earth

The most important thing is this
Have you had a second birth

Scripture

*Jesus answered and said unto him, Verily, verily,
I say unto thee, except a man be born again, he
cannot see the kingdom of heaven.
John 3:3*

*And as it is appointed unto men once to die,
but after this the judgment.
Hebrews 9:27*

The Resurrection

Hallelujah! The tomb is empty, come and see
Over death He's won the victory
He is the Son of God, who His divinity had shod
To become an ordinary man with a mission and a plan

He came to earth to redeem the human race
To take the wrath of God in our place
God's justice was satisfied
When Jesus hung his head and died

The earth shook violently and the sky turned dark
When Jesus became our saving ark
He went down into hell and gave the devil a spell
He took the key, over death and hell the victory

But, O what Joy was yet to come
When His mission here on earth was done
The light shone brighter than the day
When angels rolled the stone away
Some soldiers fled and others hid their face
When the Glory of God hit that place

He is risen! He is not here!
The angels said when Mary came
She didn't recognize her precious Lord
He didn't look the same

Are you washed in the precious blood
Are your sins forgiven
If you are not certain that you are in the Way
Then make sure and give Him your life today

 WALLI ANTONIE ZAMORANO

Scripture

*Jesus said unto her, I am the resurrection and the
life; he that believeth in me, though he were dead,
yet shall he live.*

*And whosoever liveth and believeth in me shall
never die; Believest thou this?*
John 11:25

*I am he that liveth, and was dead and behold,
I am alive for evermore, Amen; and have the keys
of hell and of death.*
Revelation 1:18

The Transformation

There is a battle, I cannot see
Going on inside of me
It is a struggle for dominion
Each one has his own opinion
I am the one who must decide
Which one of them is right

When I let the new man win
There will be Peace and Joy within
When the old man stays alive
He'll bring discontent and strife

God says, the old man must go to the cross
Your born again spirit is now the boss
Hallelujah, can you see
In Christ we'll have the victory
Old things have passed away
Behold everything is new

We must lay aside all Selfishness and Pride
Not to this world we shall be conformed
But into His image we must be transformed

Jesus will become number One
He is the Savior, God's only Son
It is only when we ask Him into our heart
This whole process of remaking us can start
The end result will be
that He will see Himself in you and me

    WALLI ANTONIE ZAMORANO

Scripture

Knowing this, that our old man is crucified with Him, that the body of sin might be destroyed, that henceforth we should not serve sin.
Romans 6:6

And be not conformed to this world, but be ye transformed by the renewing of your mind that ye may prove what is that good and acceptable and perfect will of God.
Romans 12:2

As it is written, there is none righteous, no, not one. For all have sinned and come short of the Glory of God.
Romans 3: 10, 23

Two Kingdoms

There are two kingdoms the Word of God says
The kingdom of darkness and the kingdom of light
We must choose while we live
To whom our allegiance we will give
Will we come to the light, or in the darkness hide

Let me plead with you today
Don't throw your life away
For a moment of earthly pleasure
When you may have His eternal treasure

Eternity is a very long time
It lasts forever and ever
Never, never, never can you make it right
When without the New Birth you have died

Now is the time to decide
Please put away your pride
And come to Jesus God's only Son
Who over death and the grave the victory has won
When you confess your sin and ask Him to come in
You will be born again
You'll be translated out of the kingdom of darkness
Into the kingdom of light
Your wrongs will be made right
God leaves the choice up to you and me
Where we will spend eternity

 WALLI ANTONIE ZAMORANO

Scripture

*But seek ye first the kingdom of God and his
righteousness and all these things shall be
added unto you.*
Matthew 6:33

*Who hath delivered us from the power
or darkness, and has translated us into the
kingdom of his dear son.*
Colossians 1:13

*In whom the god of this world hath blinded
the minds of them which believe not, lest the
light of the glorious gospel of Christ, who is
the image of God, should shine unto them.*
II Corinthians 4:4

Two Trees

In the midst of the Garden stood two Trees
You may not eat the fruit of one of these
God spoke to Adam and Eve. This is the reason why
If you partake of the Tree of the Knowledge
Of Good and Evil, you shall surely die

Now the serpent came to Eve and said
You shall not die, you shall be like gods instead
Eve believed the lie and took a bite
And gave to Adam who stood nearby

Their eyes were opened and it was too late
They had disobeyed and sealed their fate
God banned them from the Garden
And placed angels with flaming swords at the gate

Even before the creation of man, God knew
What Adam would do
God had already devised another plan, to rescue fallen man
He would send His only Son in the fullness of time
To make an atonement for all, who because of Adam's fall
Had become like him, stained by sin

When God made man, He did not want a puppet on a string
To be controlled by Him. He gave man a free will to choose

The Tree of Life, that was in the Garden
Has come, as His Son, our sins to pardon
God is still giving man a choice, to hearken to His voice
Which Tree will you choose? God says to us today
Accept My Son and you shall live with Me throughout eternity
Reject My Son and live a lie, all who do that must surely die

When at the judgment seat of Christ you'll stand

 WALLI ANTONIE ZAMORANO

And He is holding the book of life in his hand
Jesus will take a look, in the book
And if one's name is not found
For the Lake of Fire he is bound

While you are reading this poem, there is still time
Forgiveness from your sin to find
It is so easy, a child can understand the way
Just ask Jesus into your heart today
He is faithful and will answer your prayer
And give you a brand new start from there

All those millions that have come to Salvation
Out of every kindred and every nation
Will meet again in that great city
Coming down from above, the New Jerusalem
The Tree of Life will be there
Each month a different fruit to bear
No more restricted from man
God invites us to eat all we can
Rev 22:2, Gen 1

No Greater Love

Greater Love hath no man
than this, that a man
lay down his life for his friends.

John 15:13

About The Cross

Why doesn't anybody want
To put the cross on the altar anymore
The cross, where Jesus our iniquity bore
He took the blame, and bore the shame
For you and me, so we could go free

I know, to picture Him on the cross is hard
His body was bruised and His face was marred
His flesh was torn, where the stripes He had born
He did it for you and me, so we could go free

You say, that it tears you apart
To think about when they pierced His heart.
He was wounded for you and me, so we could go free

How excruciating must have been the pain.
Don't let Him have hung on the cross in vain
He suffered for you and for me, so we could go free

They made a mockery of Him
And with a crown of thorns made Him king
Even when the blood ran down His face
He was reaching out in Mercy and Grace
To forgive you and me, so we could go free

I will forever cling to the cross of Calvary
Where my Savior bled and died for me

Scripture

But he was wounded for our transgressions he was
bruised for our iniquities the chastisement of our
peace was upon him and with his stripes we are healed.
Isaiah 53:5

And when they had platted a crown of thorns,
to put upon his head, and a reed in his right hand,
and they bowed the knee before him, saying Hail,
King of the Jews.
Matthew 27:29

But God forbid that I should glory, save in the
cross of our Lord Jesus Christ, by whom the
world is crucified unto me and I unto the world.
Galatians 6:14

Walli Antonie Zamorano

A Hill Called Calvary

If it was not for the cross on a hill called Calvary
Where would I be
What took place on a hill called Calvary
Changed the course of history
They crucified Jesus on a tree
On a hill called Calvary

He shed His precious blood for you and me
On that cross on a hill called Calvary
The battle between good and evil, you see
Was decided on a hill called Calvary
If the devil had known the hidden mystery
He would not have crucified the Lord
On a hill called Calvary

All you can see is an empty tree
When you look back at Calvary
And you know, who won the victory
On that cross on a hill called Calvary

What happened on a hill called Calvary
Will determine every man's destiny
Jesus bought Salvation for all humanity
When He shed His blood on a hill called Calvary

There is a choice for you and me
Will we accept the finished work of Calvary
Or be lost without Christ for all eternity
By rejecting the sacrifice made
On a hill called Calvary

Scripture

*And when they were come to the place which is
called Calvary, there they crucified him, and the
malefactors, one the right hand, and the other on
the left.*
Luke 23:33

*But we speak the wisdom of God in a mystery,
even the hidden wisdom, which God ordained
before the world unto our Glory.
Which none of the princes of the world knew;
for had they known it, they would not have
crucified the Lord of Glory.*
I Corinthians 2: 7, 8

   Walli Antonie Zamorano

Another Look At Calvary

When I look at Calvary
And see Jesus hanging helplessly on that tree
I realize, that He was made of flesh just like me
O, what agony
I can hear the blow of the hammer
When they drove the nails into His hands and feet
I cannot imagine the pain He endured
So my freedom would be secured

Do you see, when they tied Him to the pole
And pulled the whip across His back
Every stroke that was laid on Him
Was so that you and I could be made whole

Like a lamb brought to the slaughter
Defenseless and without resistance
The Lamb of God went the distance
He could have called
Ten thousand angels to His assistance

They plucked out His beard and spit in His face
They pushed a crown of thorns deep into His brow
They put a purple robe on Him
And mocked Him and cried
"Look at the King of the Jews now

Yes, He went to Calvary
Paid the price in full for our iniquity
But please remember, we are His sheep
A humble and contrite spirit we must keep

Our hearts are desperately wicked and prone to sin
We must come to the Cross daily the victory to win

Scripture

*And when they were come to the place, which is
called Calvary, there they crucified him, and the
malefactors, one on the right hand and the other
on the left.*
Luke 23:33

*And they stripped him and put on him a scarlet
robe. And when they had platted a crown of
thorns, they put it upon his head, and a reed in
his right hand and they bowed the knee before
him and mocked him, saying, Hail, King of the
Jews. And they spit upon him, and took a reed
and smote him on the head.*
Matthew 27: 28-30

 WALLI ANTONIE ZAMORANO

Consider The Blood

Where would we be
If it was not for the Cross of Calvary
Only by the Blood shed by God's Son
Can we overcome
The Blood of Jesus is as powerful now
As it was way back when
Millions have been cleansed by it since then

The Blood will never lose its power
You can depend on it this very hour
Listen to what this precious Blood will do
That our Savior shed for you

It will wash away your sin and make you pure within
It will redeem everyone who will call upon the Son
It will cover and protect you
It will comfort and direct you
It will bring your wayward children home
Never more to roam

There is not enough time now or in eternity
To show our gratitude
For the price Jesus paid, to save the lost
There is no power here on earth
That can compare with its worth

Diamonds or gold cannot save a single soul
Holy, Holy, Holy is the precious Blood of Jesus
Worthy, Worthy, Worthy is the Lamb of God
Forever to be worshipped and adored
Is our glorious Redeemer, our precious Lord

Song

What can wash away my sin? Nothing but the Blood of Jesus
What can make me pure within? Nothing but the Blood of Jesus
How precious is that flow, that makes me white as snow
No other fount I know, nothing but the Blood of Jesus

SONG

The Blood that Jesus shed for me way back at Calvary
The blood that gives me strength from day to day
It will never lose its power
It reaches to the highest mountains
It flows in the lowest valley
The Blood that gives me strength from day to day
it will never lose its power

 Walli Antonie Zamorano

Glory To The Lamb

Join with me in one accord
To worship Him our risen Lord
Join with me in thankful refrain
To worship Him who was slain
Glory to the Lamb

Join with me and bow in gratitude
To worship Him who is our substitute
Join with me and let your praise arise
To worship Him who paid the price
Glory to the Lamb

Join with me in humble adoration
To worship Him who brought salvation
Join with me to honor His blood
The sin erasing cleansing flood
Glory to the Lamb

Join with me in cheerful celebrations
To worship Him who sprinkled all nations
Join with me
and let the Hallelujahs ring
To worship Him who is our King
Glory to the Lamb

Join with me to raise the banner higher
Let us worship Him
Who takes us through the fire
Join with me and shout the victory
To worship Him who has set us free

Scripture

But God commended His Love toward us in that,
while we were yet sinners, Christ
died for us.

Much more then, being now justified by his
blood, we shall be saved from wrath through him.
Romans 5: 8,9

For I am not ashamed of the gospel of Christ; for it
is the power of God unto salvation to every one
that believeth; to the Jew first, and also the Greek.
Romans 1:16

Hear The Blood Speak

Would you like to find out
What the Blood of Jesus is talking about
When Abel's blood spoke out of the ground
It was crying out that justice would be found

The Blood of Jesus speaks of better things
Its voice can be heard, but not out of the earth
Jesus sprinkled it on the altar in heaven above
Satisfying the Father's Love
It is always speaking; let's just begin to listen in

BY MY POWER there is forgiveness of sin
You can be reconciled to God a new life to begin
BY MY POWER you are delivered out of darkness
Into His marvelous light
When you put your trust in Jesus Christ

BY MY POWER healing can be found
For your body, soul and mind
By the stripes Jesus bore, when His back they tore

BY MY POWER peace with God is restored
When you confess Jesus as your Lord

BY MY POWER you have access to God's Throne
And find comfort when you feel alone
BY MY POWER you are made over comers here on earth
Defeating Satan by reminding him of the Word

Scripture

*And to Jesus the mediator of the new covenant,
and to the blood of sprinkling, that speaketh
better things than that of Abel.*
Hebrews 12:24

*And Cain talked with his brother Abel; and
it came to pass, when they were in the field
that Cain rose up against Abel his brother,
and slew him.*

*And he said, What hast thou done? the voice
of thy brother's blood crieth unto me from the
ground.*
Genesis 4:8, 10

Heaven Bound

Stop, and turn around
Come with me I'm Heaven bound
I was lost and didn't know
Where I should go
To find the answers
To the questions deep within

O, Glory to God's only Son
He was the one, I had been searching for
To quench the longing in my soul
He's the only one, who can make you whole

Stop, and turn around
Follow the Savior, I have already found
When you ask Him into your heart
He'll give you a brand new start
Old things are passed away
When He comes in to stay

O, Glory to the Father
Who sent His only Son
Our iniquities to pardon
So through the blood of Jesus
We are made into one

We are called His Bride
To rule forever at His side

Scripture

*Therefore if any man be in Christ he is a new creature,
old things are passed away, behold, all things are
become new.*
II Cor. 5:17

*For the Lord himself shall descend from heaven
with a shout , with the voice of the archangel and
with the trump of God; and the dead in Christ shall
rise first...*
I Thess.4:16

*There is one body, and one Spirit, even as ye are
called in one hope of your calling; One Lord, one
faith, one baptism, One God, and Father of all
who is above all, and through all, and all in all.*
Eph. 4:4

Highway To Holiness

Come and walk this Highway with me
It leads through the cross of Calvary
Only the redeemed of the Lord are allowed
No one is unclean in that crowd

Those who have kneeled at the cross
And confessed their sin
Who are washed in the blood
May enter therein

There is safety for you on that road
Jesus will carry your heavy load
Joy and gladness will fill your heart
If from the path you won't depart

We must walk circumspectly
Not looking to the left or right
We must keep our goal in sight
Narrow is the way that leads to life

The enemy is waiting on every turn
And on every side
Hoping for someone from the road to slide
To answer his temptations and give in
And fall back into sin

If you get distracted and stray
And veer off this Highway
You must come back through the door
And be washed in the blood once more

This Highway is within our hearts
When we are one with Him
When we love our neighbor as ourselves
Our journey of Holiness can begin

Scripture

*And an highway shall be there, and a way, and it
shall be called the way of Holiness; the unclean
shall not pass over it; but it shall be for those:
the wayfaring men though fools shall not err therein.*
Isaiah 35:8

*Who hath delivered us from the power of darkness
and has translated us into the kingdom of his dear Son.*
Colossians 1:13

*To whom God would make known what is the
riches of the Glory of this mystery among the
Gentiles; which is Christ in you the hope of Glory.*
Colossians 1:27

Hold On To The Cross

Beware of wolves in sheep's clothing
Walking about in your midst
Who say that they are your brothers
Betraying the Lord with a "Judas" kiss

They say Jesus was just a prophet
Like all the others that came along
They deny the cross and its salvation
They boast in their own interpretation

Be careful my Friend
Do not fall prey to their persuasion
They are spreading falsehood
Trying to undermine our foundation

When it comes to the truth
We must not compromise
The Gospel of Jesus Christ
By agreeing with someone's lies

We must hold on to the cross
Even if we suffer loss
The Blood of Jesus Christ
Is the only acceptable sacrifice

The Blood is the only remedy
The only way to victory
The only way to be set free
The cross of Jesus Christ
Is the power unto salvation

It is the only escape
From eternal damnation

Scripture

*For many walk, of whom I have told you often and
now tell you even weeping, that they are the enemies
of the cross of Christ.*
Philippines 3:18

*And having made peace through the blood of his cross,
by him to reconcile all things unto himself, by him I say
whether they be things on earth, or things in heaven.*
Colossians 1:20

WALLI ANTONIE ZAMORANO

It Is Getting Late

The hour is getting late
There's no more time to wait
To get ready for that fateful day
When my Son will catch His Bride away

Are you washed in the blood
Have you confessed all of your sin
Only those in white garments
Will be ushered in

There is only one way to come to Me
Its through the cross of Calvary
My Son died there and took the sin
For all humanity the victory to win

Make absolutely sure today
That your wicks are trimmed
And your lamps will burn
At the moment of My Son's return

Awake! Awake is the call
From the watchman on the wall
Make yourselves ready; is his shout
So you may enter in
And will not be left out

Look up, the hour is drawing nigh
When lightning will split the eastern sky
On a white horse My Son will ride
To catch away His chosen Bride

Scripture

*Yet you have a few people in Sardis, who have
not soiled their clothes, they will walk with me
dressed in white, for they are worthy.*
Revelation 3:4

*But while they were on there way to buy oil, the
bridegroom arrived. The virgins who were ready
walked in with him to the wedding banquet and the
door was closed.*
Matthew 25:10

*For the Lord himself will come down from heaven
with a loud command, with the voice of the archangel
and with the trumpet call of God.*
I Thess. 4: 16, 17

WALLI ANTONIE ZAMORANO

Preach The Cross

Our faith would be in vain
If we could not make the claim
That Jesus died and rose again

Mohammed and Buddha
Confucius and all the rest
Are still in the grave
And have no power to save

The eternal battle has been won
By Jesus Christ, God's only Son
The empty grave is the proof
That He is the only Truth

We must come to the cross
And believe and trust in Him
He will forgive our sin
And we shall be born again

His Word shall be our daily bread
That's how our spirit must be fed
Then our Faith will become strong
And we know that to Jesus we belong

We must reach out to the lost
And preach the cross at any cost
Then more captives will go free
And signs and wonders we shall see

Here I am, Lord send me
Your ambassador I want to be

Scripture

But he answered and said It is written, man shall not live by bread alone, but by every word that proceedeth out of the mouth of God.
Matthew 4:4

Give us this day our daily bread.
Matthew 6:11

And Jesus said unto her, touch me not; for I am not yet ascended to my Father; but go to my brethren, and say unto them, I ascend unto my Father, and your Father; and to my God, and your God.
John 20:17

 Walli Antonie Zamorano

Remember The Blood

O, can you see, the Lamb up on the tree
It is Jesus shedding His Blood for you and me
This is the hour, when we will need its power
If it had not been for Calvary

Humanity would have been lost for all eternity
Millions have been cleansed from their sin,
Reconciled by the Blood, a new life to begin

Jesus said, when I'll be lifted up on that tree
All men will be drawn unto me
O, can't you see, without the Blood where would we be
Jesus endured the cross, so we would not be lost

This miracle of new life can only begin
When we invite Him to come in
His Blood has power, its like taking an inward shower
It'll wash our sins away
So His Holy Spirit can come in to stay
Then we'll be changed into His image from day to day

Remember, when the price in full He had paid
Taken down from the cross and in the tomb was laid
He went to hell and took the keys
And through the blood of His cross He made peace

On the third day He came out of the grave
And the authority over the enemy to us He gave
So, when the enemy comes in like a flood
He must flee at the mention of Jesus' Blood

Scripture

How much more shall the blood of Christ, who offered himself without spot to God, purge your conscience from dead works to serve the living God.
Hebrews 9:14

And it is appointed unto man once to die and after that the judgment.
Hebrews 9:27

And having made peace through the blood of his cross, by him to reconcile all things unto himself; by him, I say, whether they be the things in earth, or things in heaven.
Colossians 1:20

WALLI ANTONIE ZAMORANO

Remember The Cross

One day in the Word I read
If any man will come after me
Let him deny himself
Take up his "cross" and follow me

I know, on a hill called Calvary
My Savior bled and died for me
On a rugged cross was nailed
Over sin and death prevailed

He despised the shame
And endured the pain
That throughout all eternity
The Joy set before Him we would be

The cross is empty now
Yet it reminds us still
That in obedience to the Father
Jesus laid down His will

Just as Jesus gave himself
An offering for my sin
I must deny my selfish ways
The victory to win.

Daily I must pick up my 'cross'
My Faith has to be tried
Until there's no more dross
And my vessel is purified

Scripture

*And he that taketh not his cross and followeth after
me, is not worthy of me.
Matthew 10:38*

*Looking unto Jesus, the author and finisher of our faith;
who for the Joy that was set before him, endured the cross,
despising the shame, and is set down at the right hand
of the throne of God.
Hebrews 12:2*

Take Up Your Cross

When I kneel down to pray
I am reminded of the cross each day
And of the blood of Jesus
Whose miracle working power never ceases

When we take up our cross and die
And wholly on the Lord rely
We will see miracles galore
And greater works than before

So, take up your cross and come up the hill
With a pure heart and a surrendered will
Your hands must be clean
And a contrite spirit must be seen

Every day we must pick up our cross
And count the cost
Not my will Lord, but thine be done
Help me Lord, my race to run

The message of the cross has not changed
It is still the only power unto salvation
For every one and every nation
God himself counted the cost
When He sent His Son to die for the lost

God is looking down from above
For those who've died to self and walk in love
Who are over comers, who He can trust
And with signs and wonders

Into the final harvest thrust

Scripture

*For thus saith the high and lofty One that
inhabiteth eternity, whose Name is holy;
I dwell in the high and holy place, with him also
who is of a contrite and humble spirit, to revive
the spirit of the humble and to revive the heart
of the contrite ones.
Isaiah 57:15*

*Who shall ascend into the hill of the Lord?
or who shall stand in his holy place?
He that hath clean hands, and a pure heart; who
hath not lifted up his soul unto vanity, nor sworn
deceitfully.
Psalm 24: 3*

The Gospel

When people ask you: What do you believe
Why are you so certain and why do you never doubt
Just let them know, what the Gospel is all about

It is all about the CROSS, where our Savior died
When they nailed Him there, our iniquities to bear

Its all about the BLOOD, Jesus shed on the tree
It has the power to cleanse from sin this very hour

Its all about His GLORY, the angels told the story
Joy to the world has come, when God sent His only Son

It is all about SALVATION
To rescue man from damnation
When you hear His voice, remember
He's giving you the choice
Be smart and ask Him into your heart

It is all about God's KINGDOM
We pray that it will come
The one who came to atone will sit upon the throne
All war will cease. There will be everlasting peace

It is all about JESUS
He's the LAMB
That was slain and shall forever reign
He is the WAY, the TRUTH and the LIFE
He is the BEGINNING and the END
Eternity with Him we'll spend

Scripture

Moreover brethren I declare unto you the gospel which I preached unto you, which also you have received, and wherein ye stand.

By which ye are saved, if ye keep in memory what I preached unto you unless ye have believed in vain.
I Corinthians 15:1,2

For whosoever shall call upon the Name of the Lord shall be saved.
Romans 10:13

Having therefore, brethren boldness to enter into the holiest by the blood of Jesus.
Hebrews 10:19

WALLI ANTONIE ZAMORANO

The Mystery Of Redemption

When God made Adam and Eve and put them in the Garden
They had no need of a pardon
Their hearts were innocent, and their blood was pure
With the Master they daily talked
And in obedience to Him they walked

Until one day they listened to a lie, You shall not surely die
The serpent said, You shall be like gods instead
Adam and Eve ate the fruit of the tree that was forbidden
And they could not stay hidden
Through this act of disobedience, sin entered the human race
And man fell from Grace
An innocent lamb had to be slain, to temporarily cover the stain

Before the world began, God had already devised a plan
To redeem man from damnation and to grant him His Salvation
Without the shedding of blood, there is no remission of sin
It is the only way the victory to win

In the fullness of time God sent His Son
Born of a virgin an obedient one
Jesus was the only one who qualified
When on a rugged cross He died
He shed His sinless blood for you and me
This is the mystery
When we confess our sin and ask Him in
Our blood is washed and we are pure again

Forever grateful I will be
For His Salvation so rich and free
Just like a seed planted into the ground
Has to die, to bring forth fruit and multiply
So Jesus Christ through His sacrifice
Has brought many sons to Glory

Scripture

*But God commendeth his love toward us in that
while we were yet sinners, Christ died for us.*
Romans 5:8

*The wages of sin is death; but the gift of God is
eternal life through Jesus Christ our Lord.*
Romans 6:23

*If we confess our sins, he is faithful and just
to forgive us for our sins and cleanse us from all
unrighteousness.*
I John 1:9

The Power Of The Blood

The blood of Christ alone can for our sins atone
No deep repentance can remove the stain
All of man's efforts to be forgiven are in vain
When God breathed into man, his life here on this earth began
Man was to live in obedience to Him, and not give in
To the devil's clever lie
God had warned him, if he did, he would surely die

When the fullness of time had come
He sent His only Son
To die for the sin of everyone

Jesus is the Lamb
Slain from the world's foundation
To sprinkle His blood on every nation
Through Jesus' blood alone
We have access to the throne

We may boldly come before the King
Our offering of praise to bring
Our bodies are His temple made of clay
Where the Holy Spirit comes in to stay

O, how we need to thank Him every day
His blood keeps washing our sins away
O, Hallelujah, come let us sing
And dance before our King

There is power in Jesus' blood
Millions have been washed in its cleansing flood
His blood will wash you whiter than the snow
Repent! Ask Him in, and you too will know

Scripture

*And almost all things are by the law purged with
blood and without shedding of blood is no remission.*
Hebrews 9:22

*Having therefore boldness, brethren to enter into the
holiest by the blood of Jesus.*
Hebrews 10:19

*Whom God has set forth to be a propitiation through
faith in His blood, to declare his righteousness through
remission of sins that are past, through the forbearance
of God.*
Romans 3:25

The Power Of The Cross

Paul says in his exhortation
The Cross is the power unto salvation
The Cross is the divider of time and the divider men
It is the signpost at the crossroad of our life

Where our future we must decide
The road to heaven is narrow
And few there are that find the way
The highway to hell is broad
And looks like fun and play

Long before Jesus died for all mankind
The Cross was already on the Father's mind
He could see, His Son up on a tree
Defeating the old serpent, the enemy
He told Moses to lift up a serpent on a pole
And the people that looked upon it
were made whole
When Jesus died on the Cross
This scripture was fulfilled
That by His stripes we are healed

The victory over the enemy is ours
Because of what Jesus did
He spoiled all principalities and powers
Triumphing over them in It
Satan has been defeated. Jesus took the key
It all happened on the cross of Calvary

When the first settlers came ashore
Their dependency on God they swore
They planted a Cross in the sand
And to God they dedicated this land
If you want to be made new
There is room at the Cross for you

Scripture

*Being found in the fashion as a man he humbled
himself, and became obedient unto death, even
the death on the cross.*
Philippians 2:8

*Enter ye in at the strait gate; for wide is the gate
and broad is the way, that leadeth to destruction
and many there be that go in thereat.
Because strait is the gate, and narrow is the way,
which leadeth unto life, and few there be that find it.*
Matthew 7:13,14

 WALLI ANTONIE ZAMORANO

They Did Not Know

Can you see
The devil and his cohorts rejoicing with glee
When they saw Jesus hanging on the tree

They did not know
When Jesus sweat great drops of blood in the garden
It was so the trespasses of our souls He could pardon

They did not know
When the blood dripped down from the thorny crown
It was so cleansing for our mind
Through the precious blood of Jesus we could find

They did not know
When they drove the nails into His feet
That the blood would guarantee the enemy's defeat
He can't stop us from spreading the
Word until everyone has heard

They did not know
When they thrust the spear into Jesus' side
That the blood and water that gushed out
Would wash and sanctify His eternal Bride

They did not know
That Jesus Christ from the grave would rise
If the princes of this world would have known
They would not have crucified the Lord of Glory
For the mystery of the redemption story
Was hidden from them

From before the world began
Glory to the Lamb

Scripture

Which none of the princes of this world knew;
for had they known, they would not have crucified
the Lord of Glory.

I Corinthians 2:8
And being in agony He prayed more earnestly
and his sweat was as if it were great drops of
blood falling down to the ground.
Luke 22:44

When they had platted a crown of thorns they
put it upon his head, and a reed in his right
hand; and they bowed their knee before him,
saying Hail, King of the Jews.
Matthew 27:29

Walli Antonie Zamorano

Blow The Trumpet

*Blow the trumpet in Zion and
sound an alarm in my holy mountain:
let all the inhabitants of the land
tremble; for the Day of the Lord
cometh, for it is nigh at hand.*

Joel 2:1

After The Harvest

When the Great Tribulation is over
And the Harvest has come in
The New Millennium will begin
The heavens will rend
And My Son will descend

When you see Him
He will not come as the Lamb
He will come as Judah's Lion
He will sit on David's throne
And He will rule out of Zion

All war will cease. He will bring Peace
The weapons that were used before
Will not be needed any more

There will be great jubilation
When the people from the remaining nations
Will come up each year to Jerusalem
To take part in the joyful celebration

From the four corners of the earth they will come
The gates of the city will be open to everyone
Thank offerings they will bring
Singing Holy, Holy, Holy is the King

Jerusalem , shall be called the city of the Lord
The Zion of the Holy One of Israel
Of her Glory everyone will tell

 WALLI ANTONIE ZAMORANO

Scripture

And he said, The Lord shall roar out of Zion and utter his voice from Jerusalem,..
Amos 1: 2

And many nations shall come and say, Come let us go up to the mountain of the Lord, and to the house of the God of Jacob; and he will teach us his ways, and we will walk in his paths; for the law shall go forth of Zion, and the Word of the Lord from Jerusalem.
Micah 4:2

All In Jesus' Name

When revival has come
The greater works shall be done
By those who believe in the Son

The blind will see, the deaf will hear
All in Jesus' Name
The lame will walk, the dumb will talk
All in Jesus' Name

When revival has come
Great exploits shall be wrought
By those who know their God

The dead are raised, the lost are saved
All in Jesus' Name
The sick are healed, demons revealed
All in Jesus' Name

When revival has come
People will speak in other tongues
Filled with the Holy Spirits power
They will prophesy, they will testify
All in Jesus Name

They shall overcome
By the blood of the Lamb
All in Jesus Name

His Name is exalted above all others
Come let us praise His Name

WALLI ANTONIE ZAMORANO

Scripture

Verily, verily I say unto you, He that believeth
on me the works that I do shall he do also; and
greater works than these shall he do; because
I go unto my Father.
John 14:12

And such as do wickedly against the covenant shall
be corrupt by flatteries; but the people that do
know their God shall be strong, and do exploits.
Daniel 11:32

Believe And Receive

The promises of God remain
There is the sound of an abundance of rain
In the latter days He will pour out His spirit on everyone
Are you ready to believe, is your heart prepared to receive

Are your eyes open, can you see
The splendor of His Majesty
When you look up into the sky
You might see a star shoot by
You become speechless when you behold
How the millions of stars and galaxies unfold
His magnificent creation is perfectly positioned in space
To support the existence of the human race

Can you believe? Can you comprehend
That this awesome Creator of heaven and earth
Would limit himself to a human birth
Jesus demonstrated His Love
When He laid down the Glory he had above
To submit to a cruel death on a tree
To be crucified at Calvary

The curtain has been rent
His Shekinah Glory will descend
His cleansing fire He will send
Every one will fall down and repent

My question is this, How can anyone miss
The fulfillment of prophecy
The Glory of His creation
And the invitation to eternal Salvation

There is a judgment for all of us some day
The cross of Jesus is the only way

 WALLI ANTONIE ZAMORANO

Scripture

And it shall come to pass afterwards that I will pour out of my spirit upon all flesh, and your sons and your daughters shall prophesy, your old men shall dream dreams, and your young men shall see visions.
Joel 3:28

In the beginning God created the heaven and the earth.
Genesis 1:1

Blow The Trumpet

Blow the trumpet in the land
The Lord's return is now at hand
Kingdoms rise and kingdoms fall
The Church of Christ is standing tall

Just as the river rushes toward the sea
You cannot stop its flow
Assuredly
So the returning of the Son of Man shall be
The Word of God says so
Just as a woman travails in labor for her child
She cannot stop the baby's birth
Assuredly
So the returning of the Son of Man shall be
As He went up, so He will return back to earth
Assuredly
So the returning of the Son of Man shall be
He'll establish His kingdom in victory
Just as harvest will follow the sowing of seed
As God established it and it was decreed
Assuredly
So the returning of the Son of Man shall be
It was planned by the Father before eternity

The signs are all around, so listen to the sound
The time is drawing near
When the trumpet you will hear
And in the clouds HE shall appear
Day follows every night

As darkness is disbursed by light

 WALLI ANTONIE ZAMORANO

Scripture

For the Lord himself will come down from heaven,
with a loud command, with the voice of the archangel
and with the trumpet of God.
I Thess. 4:16, 17

At that time they will see the Son of Man coming
in a cloud with power and great Glory.
Luke 21:27

Harvest Time

Arise and shine, all who are Mine
My Glory you will see, when you come and follow Me
I'll make you fishers of men in the sea of humanity
There are many more waiting at its shore
Who have not heard My life giving Word before

All you, young and old, short and tall
Can you hear His call
The hour is late, you must not hesitate
Just go and obey, He'll give you the words to say
There is no need to plow
The fields are ready for the harvest now

Don't resist, it is time to enlist
From east to west and south to north
The army of the Lord is going forth
When the Good News has been preached
And every nation has been reached
He will close the door.
Reconciliation will be no more

For all those who have been born again
The glorious Millennium will begin
And Jesus the Messiah will reign as King

Will you be there
When the marriage supper of the Lamb
We will share

 Walli Antonie Zamorano

Scripture

*Arise, shine, for thy light has come and
the glory of the Lord is risen upon thee.*
Isaiah 60:1

*Blessed and holy is he that has part in the first
resurrection, on such the second death has no
power, but they shall be priests of God and of
Christ, and shall reign with him a thousand years.*
Revelation 20:6

Latter Days

Yes, My shaking shall come
It has already begun
Nations that have been
Shall not be seen
I will set up and I will pull down
I am the Lord of Hosts, the Renown

When their desire has come
And the people are as one
Calling unto Me night and day
And have turned from their wicked way
Then My Glory will descend
And cover the earth from end to end

The glory of the latter house
Shall exceed the one before
And war shall be no more
My Peace shall be in that place
Where My people humble themselves
And seek My face

I am the Lord of Hosts, your God
I am the one you have sought
I am mighty in the midst of you
I will bring you safely through

Do not be afraid
When the earth begins to quake
And everything begins to shake
In the latter days it must be
To purge the world from iniquity
So that the Millennium can come
Governed by My Son

     WALLI ANTONIE ZAMORANO

Scripture

The Lord thy God in the midst of thee is mighty,
he will save, he will rejoice over thee with joy;
he will rest in his love, he will joy over thee with
singing.
Zephaniah 3:17

For thus saith the Lord of hosts; Yet a little while
and I will shake the heavens and the earth and the
sea and the dry land.
And I will shake all nations and the desire of all
nations shall come; and I will fill this house with
glory saith the Lord of hosts...
Haggai 2:6, 7

Listen To The Sound

Lift up your heads and listen to the sound
My latter rain is falling to the ground
Drops of Mercy and drops of Grace
Are gently landing on each face

Lift up your heads and listen to the sound
The wind of My Spirit is blowing all around
To fan the flame and blow the chaff away
So no filth and worldliness may stay

Lift up your heads and listen to the sound
It is the roar of fire coming from the mount
To consume the living sacrifice, offered up to Me
To purify My vessels and give them victory

Lift up your heads and listen to the sound
Instead of tears and sorrow
Joy and gladness will abound
My bride is getting ready for that glorious day
When Gabriel blows the trump
And she'll be caught away

Scripture

*Ask of the Lord rain in the time of the latter rain;
so the Lord shall make bright clouds, and give
them showers of rain, to everyone grass in the field.
Zechariah 10:1*

*Then the fire of the Lord fell and consumed the
burnt sacrifice and the wood, and the stones and
the dust and licked up the water that was in the
trench.
I Kings 18:38*

Messiah Has Come

Hear, O Israel
Your Messiah has already come
He is God's only Son
He is the Lamb, God provided for Abraham

He died and rose again. He is the offering
That can wash away our sin
His precious Blood alone can for our sins atone

Messiah will come again to rule His own
He alone is worthy to sit on David's throne

He is the King of kings and Lord of lords
Father, Spirit and Son
O Israel, Your God is One

When you lift up your voice
And call on Him, He will come in
He will save your soul
And make you whole

Blow the trumpet in Zion
Roar O Judah's Lion
And let everyone hear
That Messiah's return is near

Rejoice, and be glad
You must no longer be sad
Your deliverance has come
Through Messiah, God's only Son

 WALLI ANTONIE ZAMORANO

Scripture

*And Abraham called the name of that place
Jehovah-Jireh; as it said to this day, In the
mount of the Lord it shall be seen.*
Genesis 22:14

*The Lord himself shall descend from heaven
with a shout, with the voice of the archangel
and the trump of God and the dead in Christ
shall rise first.*

*Then we which are alive and remain shall be
caught up together with them in the clouds
to meet the Lord in the air, and so shall we
ever be with the Lord.*
I Thess. 5:16,17

Only Overcomers

I have called you to be an overcomer
An overcomer you must be
Only overcomers will have the victory

With the world you must be through
If great exploits you want to do
You must walk in love
And keep your mind on things above

Even in a time of war
You can let your spirit soar
Above every trial and test
You can enter into My rest

With the affairs of this life
You must be done
It is by the blood of My Son
That you shall overcome

Your testimony must be sure
Your hearts must be pure
To walk in overcoming power
In this final hour

The return of My Son is at hand
Gabriel is waiting for My command
To blow the trumpet
And summon the saints from every land

Only overcomers will be allowed
To go up into the cloud
Repent and be renewed in your mind
So you will not be left behind

 Walli Antonie Zamorano

Scripture

*He that overcometh I will make a pillar in the temple
of my God; and he will go no more out, and I will
write upon him the name of my God and the name of
the city of my God, which is New Jerusalem, which
cometh down out of heaven from my God and I will
write upon him my new name.*
Revelation 3:12

*And they overcame him by the blood of the Lamb
and the word of their testimony and they loved not
their lives unto the death.*
Revelation 12:11

Our Finest Hour

This is our finest hour
The church is moving in power
This is the demonstration
A witness to every nation
The Gospel of Jesus Christ
Is the only way to Salvation

We must give ourselves
To fasting and praying
And to preaching the Word
We must walk in Love
And be endued
With power from above

Then we must go out
And heal the sick
Raise the dead
And set the captives free
For all the world to see

O, what a day it will be
When we fulfill our destiny
Selfishness will disappear
To the Lord we're drawing near
No more blemish
Conformed into His image

We will watch and pray
Until that final day
When the trumpet blows
And this mortal body
Will put on immortality

    Walli Antonie Zamorano

Scripture

And these signs shall follow them that believe,
in my Name shall they cast out devils, they shall
speak with new tongues;
They shall take up serpents; and if they drink any
deadly thing, it shall not hurt them; they shall lay
hands on the sick and they shall recover.
Mark 16:17,18

Watch therefore, for ye know not what hour your
Lord doth come.
Matthew 24:42

Power For The Final Hour

Show us Your Glory, The young people shout
We need Your Spirit to be poured out

In the book of Acts we see the gifts were working perfectly
Lets take a look and find out, what their secret was all about
We can clearly see, they walked in fear and humility
Thanking God for everything
Continuously worshipping and praising Him

You must spend more time fasting and praying
Is what the Lord is saying
Take up your cross and follow me
And My Glory you will see

When you leave the pleasures of this world behind
And get free from all the things that bind
And let My Word transform your mind
Then My hidden treasures
Of wisdom and knowledge you will find

Obedience to what God says, seems to be the key
If great exploits we want to see
We're in the final hour. We must walk in greater power

When the message of the Gospel we will preach
And the principles of the Kingdom teach
Then signs and wonders will follow the Word
And the knowledge of the Glory of the Lord
Will cover the earth

  WALLI ANTONIE ZAMORANO

Scripture

For the earth shall be filled with the knowledge
of the Glory of the Lord, as the waters cover the sea.
Habakkuk 2:14

Then Jesus beholding him loved him, and said
unto him, one thing thou lackest; go thy way,
sell whatsoever thou hast and give to the poor,
and thou shalt have treasure in heaven, and
come, take up your cross and follow me.
Mark 10:21

Restoration

God will restore
Make all things like they were before
When you repent of what you've done
Refreshing times will come
From the presence of His Son

When Jesus came to earth
His own people did not see
That He was God's Son
Who had come to set them free

They were blind
They had closed their mind
But in the latter days
God will lift the veil from their face

Then they will behold
The One of whom the scripture told
That the One they'd been waiting for
Had visited them before

The cross will be revealed to all
Jew or Gentile, great or small
Their eyes will be opened and
They'll realize
It was Messiah they had crucified

Through the blood of the cross
Jew and Gentile reconciled
In Him becoming one new man
Just like it all began

Scripture

Repent therefore and be converted, that your sins may be blotted out, when the times of refreshing shall come from the presence of the Lord; And he shall send Jesus Christ, which before was preached unto you:
Whom the heaven must receive until the times of restitution of all things, which God hath spoken by the mouth of his holy prophets since the world began.

Acts 3: 19-21

See Him Coming

There are no adequate words, that I could find
In the imagination of my mind
To describe the Glory of our coming King

In awe and wonder we will stare at the brilliant glare
When in the clouds He shall appear
With His angels drawing near
Everyone will behold, what in the Word is told

The trumpet will make the sound to be heard all around
The archangel will shout, and take those who are ready out
In a second, in the twinkling of an eye
Our bodies will be soaring into the sky
Not to be pulled by earth's gravity, but being totally set free

Soon the earth will be far behind, appearing like a little marble
Shining in the dark, as on our journey upward we embark
Oh, how glorious the gates appear as we are drawing near
Our earthly mind would blow at the brilliant glow

Hallelujah, I am so glad to find that
My earthly body stayed behind
You will be totally amazed when you behold
The streets are really made of gold
This is when I awoke out of my dream
Just when I saw the golden gleam
And in the distance I heard them sing
And glorious Hallelujahs ring

 WALLI ANTONIE ZAMORANO

Scripture

For as the lightning cometh out of the east, and
shineth even unto the west; so shall also the
coming of the Son of man be.
Matthew 24:27

For the Lord himself shall descend from heaven
with a shout, with the voice of the arch-angel,
and with the trump of God; and the dead in
Christ shall rise first.

Then we which are alive and remain shall be
caught up together with them in the clouds, to
meet the Lord in the air; and so shall we ever
be with the Lord.
I Thess. 4:16, 17

Sound The Alarm

What will you do
When dark clouds gather over you
Will you hide
Or in the shadow of My wings abide

Blow the trumpet! Sound the alarm
If you hide yourself in Me
You will not be harmed
The earth will quake the mountains move
Everything will shake at My reproof

I am your strength, your high tower
Trust in Me this very hour
Get under My wing there is room for you
Deliverance I'll bring, I'll guide you through

There is a hiding place prepared for all
Who will seek My face both great and small
It is in the secret place where you must abide
It is in My embrace, you can safely hide

I am the rock of your salvation
I am the strength of your life
I have called you out of darkness
Into My marvelous light
Do not be afraid of sudden fear
Just draw near. My Word is true
My angels are watching over you

 Walli Antonie Zamorano

Scripture

The Lord is my rock, my strength and my deliverer;
my God is my rock, in whom I take refuge. He is my
shield and the horn of my Salvation, my stronghold.
Psalm 18:2

The earth trembled and quaked, and the foundations
of the mountains shook they trembled because, He
was angry.
Psalm 18:7

But you are a chosen people, a royal priesthood, a
holy nation, a people belonging to God, that you may
declare the Praises of Him, who has delivered you out
of darkness into His wonderful light.
I Peter 2:9

The Hour Is Late

The hour is late; There is no time to wait
Fret not yourselves concerning things
And the comfort that prosperity brings
The time has come; and it is now
The harvest is ripe; no more need to plow

The hour is late
Many more must come through the narrow gate
Be not occupied with things the world has supplied
Earthly treasures will decay, only
What is done by My Spirit will stay

The hour is late
You must get rid of jealousy and hate
An abundance of Joy and Peace
I leave with all of these who obey My command
And reach out with a helping hand
Those who take heed of the hour
Will walk in My Love and Power

The hour is late; Please don't hesitate
Hurry into the streets and compel them to come
Even though they are the least
I'll invite them to My wedding feast

Don't quit until the net is full
I'll call others to help you pull
The hour will be too late
When I come through the Eastern Gate

 WALLI ANTONIE ZAMORANO

Scripture

*Go ye therefore in to the highways, and as many
as ye shall find, bid them to the marriage.*
Matthew 22:9

*Because strait is the gate, and narrow is the way,
which leadeth unto life, and few there be that find it.*
Matthew 7:14

*But seek ye first the kingdom of God and His
righteousness, and all these things shall be added
unto you.*
Matthew 6:33

The Latter Rain

Can you hear the sound
Of the abundance of rain falling to the ground
When My church comes into complete unity
Will seek My face and worship Me
Then I will come down to you as the early morning dew
There I will command the blessing - Life everlasting
You may receive it for the asking

I will make bright clouds for you
And give you showers of rain too
Times of refreshing will I send
To all those who from their sins repent

Just as the rain comes down from heaven and waters the seed
So shall my Word proceed. It shall not return void to Me
Its effectiveness will not cease
It shall accomplish what I please
Just like the bud breaks through the earth
So My Word shall bring forth the new birth

Get ready for some stormy weather
When I'll send the former and the latter rain together
It will not just be a shower. It will be a deluge of My Power
The lame shall walk, the blind shall see
Multitudes will be drawn to Me
What a glorious ingathering that shall be
Then the trump will sound from Heaven. Time has run out
The archangel will give a shout
All the saints will be rising into the air
Singing, Hallelujah, we'll have a meeting over there

 WALLI ANTONIE ZAMORANO

Scripture

*Then shall we know, if we follow on to know the Lord:
his going forth is prepared as the morning; and he shall
come unto us as the rain, as the latter and the former rain
unto the earth.*
Hosea 6:3

*Be glad then ye children of Zion, and rejoice in the
Lord your God; for he hath given you the former rain
moderately, and he will cause to come down for you
the rain, the former rain, and the latter rain in the
first month.*
Joel 2:23

There Is Coming A Day

There is coming a day, when the sky will roll away
Every eye will behold, what in the Word of God is told

Accompanied by millions of saints
The King of Kings and Lord of Lords
Will burst through the clouds as the archangel shouts

Surrounded by brilliant light
On a beautiful white stallion He will ride
Every eye will see the Glory of His Majesty

It is the One they had crucified
He is coming back to receive His bride
Those who have come to Salvation
Out of every kindred and every nation

It is a day of joy and agony as the people realize
That everything is true, that was prophesied

Today, God is calling out to you, make haste
Come to me, there is no time to waste
So when the Day is here, you will not be gripped with fear

He is God of everyone, Jew or Gentile , all may come
To receive reconciliation through the blood of Jesus
the Messiah, God's only Son

Don't be left behind! While salvation you may still find
When you give your life to Him, He'll forgive your sin
And you'll reign forever with the King

 WALLI ANTONIE ZAMORANO

Scripture

*And then shall appear the sign of the Son of man
in heaven: and then shall all tribes of the earth
mourn, and they shall see the Son of man coming
in the clouds of heaven with power and great glory.
Matt 24:30*

*In whom we have redemption through his blood,
the forgiveness of sins, according to the riches of
his grace.
Ephesians 1:7*

There Is A Sound

There's a sound coming from afar
Its the sound of the Shofar
Calling me to come apart

There's a sound coming into my ear
Its the sound of angel's wings drawing near

There's a sound coming from above
Its the cooing of the dove
Singing of the Father's love

There's a still small voice
Coming from inside
Its the Good Shepherd telling me
Everything will be alright

There's a sound coming from the throne
Like mighty rushing waters
Singing, worship Him alone

There's a shout loud and clear
It's the angel crying, Come up here

 WALLI ANTONIE ZAMORANO

Scripture

And when he putteth forth his own sheep he goeth before them, and the sheep follow him, for they know his voice.
John 10:4

After this I looked, and behold, a door was opened in heaven; and the first voice which I heard was as it were as of a trumpet talking with me; Which said, Come up hither, and I will shew thee things which must be hereafter.
Revelation 4:1

Times Of Refreshing

Are you ready to fly
Spread your wings and He'll lift you high
Are you ready to soar
He'll take you, where you've never been before

The Lord is calling you into the secret place
Of worship and praise
He'll touch you with His holy fire
And lift your spirit higher and higher
When you leave the world behind
Sweet communion at His feet you'll find
A new anointing He will pour on you
Like the early morning dew

Heaven's gates are open wide
Out of them flows the river of life
It is flooding the whole earth
People receiving the new birth
Joy and laughter is filling the air
Revival is starting everywhere

Can you hear the music playing
Can you see the people swaying
They are dancing before the Lord
lifting their voices in one accord

Angels are drawing near
Times of refreshing
From the presence of the Lord are here

 Walli Antonie Zamorano

Scripture

*Repent ye therefore and be converted, that your
sins may be blotted out, when the times of
refreshing shall come from the presence
of the Lord.*
Acts 3:19

*Be patient therefore, brethren, unto the coming of
the Lord. Behold the husbandman waiteth for the
precious fruit of the earth, and has long patience
for it, until he receive the early and the latter rain.*
James 5:7

Trim Your Wicks

Trim your wicks today
Let no worldliness stay
That your lamps may burn
At My Son's return

Don't let your flame go out
Before you hear the shout
You'll be turned away
On His wedding day

Stay filled with My Spirit
Let the whole world hear it
That Jesus died
To give men the light

His blood bought salvation
For every nation
So He may gather a spotless bride
To reign forever at His side

So cleanse your heart
And come apart
Incline your ear
So the trumpet you may hear

 WALLI ANTONIE ZAMORANO

Scripture

*Then shall the kingdom of heaven be likened unto
ten virgins, which took their lamps and went forth
to meet the bridegroom. And five of them were wise,
and five were foolish. They that were foolish took
their lamps and took no oil with them. But the wise
took oil in their vessels with their lamps. While the
bridegroom tarried, they all slumbered and slept.
And at midnight there was a cry made, Behold, the
bridegroom cometh; go ye out to meet him. Then
all those virgins arose, and trimmed their lamps
and the foolish said unto the wise, give us of your
oil, for our lamps are gone out.*
Matthew 25:1-7